What does the Bible say about leadership? If you've ever asked that question, this book is for you. Tom Harper unpacks the fundamentals of leadership and gives us biblical grounding for what healthy, God-honoring leadership looks like. He'll challenge and broaden your view of servant leadership and equip you with a biblical framework for high-performance leadership.

*Jenni Catron*
*Author, speaker, and founder of The 4Sight Group*

What are you called to achieve as a servant leader? *Servant Leader Strong* will drive you to get after your goals fervently, excellently, and biblically. In these pages, you'll find verse after verse that will build you up and fill you with the confidence that Jesus is standing right next to you—because he is!

*Kyle Idleman*
*Author of* not a fan *and* Don't Give Up

Tom Harper's new book *Servant Leader Strong* is the perfect book to take your leadership to the next level. Harper brilliantly takes a deep dive into Scripture to show the congruency between being a strong leader and also one that serves. In short, this book will inspire you and encourage you to lead more like Jesus—enough said!

*Dave Ferguson*
*Author of* Hero Maker: Five Essential Practices
for Leaders to Multiply Leaders

Aslan is not safe, but he is good. The servant leader is meek but not weak. Tom Harper's *Servant Leader Strong* offers a biblically dense regimen to build up the core strength of a true servant leader. I believe this is an invaluable resource for the leader intent on eternal success.

*Mike Sharrow*
*CEO, The C12 Group*

D0643180

In *Servant Leader Strong*, Tom Harper provides a biblical roadmap for navigating the tension of leading as a servant in all dimensions of our lives. The book was convicting and calibrating for my leadership personally and professionally. Tom is my go-to advisor for faith and work!

*Daniel Montgomery*
*CEO of Leadership Reality and author of* How to Be Present in an Absent World: A Leader's Guide to Showing Up, Paying Attention, and Becoming Fully Human

Tom asked me to write a short endorsement for this book. I agreed because I know Tom writes good stuff and so I was happy to support his new work. What I didn't realize is how much I needed to read what I would be endorsing. This helpful book came at a great time in my personal leadership journey. I found some real encouragement. You will also.

*Ron Edmondson*
*CEO, Leadership Network*

Filled with Scripture, this book is a practical theology of servant leadership. I'd encourage you to read it slowly, think through the Scripture carefully, and allow God to work it into your life. A chapter a week will give you several weeks in God's Word on the topic of strong servant leadership. Practical, challenging, and a fresh look at biblical leadership . . . I commend this book to you.

*Dr. Dann Spader*
*Author of* 4 Chair Discipling: What Jesus Calls Us to Do *(part of the Like Jesus series)*

TOM R. HARPER

# SERVANT LEADER *Strong*

## UNITING BIBLICAL WISDOM AND HIGH-PERFORMANCE LEADERSHIP

SERVANT LEADER STRONG
Uniting Biblical Wisdom and High-Performance Leadership

Tom R. Harper
Copyright © 2019 by Tom R. Harper
DeepWater Books
13100 Eastpoint Park Blvd.
Louisville, KY 40223

All rights reserved solely by the author. The author guarantees all contents are original and do not infringe on the legal rights of any other person or work. No part of this book may be reproduced in any form without the permission of the author.

ISBN 978-0-9994671-1-4

Unless otherwise indicated, all Scripture quotations are taken from The Holy Bible, New International Version® NIV®. Copyright © 1973, 1978, 1984, 2011 by Biblica, Inc.™ Used by permission. All rights reserved worldwide.

Scripture quotations marked (NLT) are taken from the Holy Bible, New Living Translation, copyright © 1996, 2004, 2015 by Tyndale House Foundation. Used by permission of Tyndale House Publishers, Inc., Carol Stream, Illinois 60188. All rights reserved.

Scripture quotations marked (MSG) are taken from *THE MESSAGE*, copyright © 1993, 2002, 2018 by Eugene H. Peterson. Used by permission of NavPress. All rights reserved. Represented by Tyndale House Publishers, Inc.

Printed in the United States of America

For Karen—A wife of noble character, a strong servant of the Lord, and a gift to all who know her.

The greatest among you will be your servant.

*—Matthew 23:11*


Now, Lord, consider their threats and enable your servants to speak your word with great boldness.

*—Acts 4:29*

# Contents

# CONTENTS

# CONTENTS

CONTENTS

# Preface

> "Whoever wants to become great among you
> must be your servant, and whoever wants to be
> first must be servant of all."
>
> —*Mark 10:43b–44*

What does "servant leadership" mean to you? Best-selling books and online media portray it as humbly meeting people's needs, but they leave out things like sacrifice, boldness, and risk. Of course, they also leave out God.

Perhaps it's wise to visit the roots of the servanthood movement for some perspective. Robert K. Greenleaf introduced us to the concept in his groundbreaking 1970 essay, "The Servant as Leader." He writes, "The servant-leader is servant first. . . . Then conscious choice brings one to aspire to lead."

In the ensuing decades, servant leadership spread into our vernacular. Several books, such as *Lead Like Jesus* by Ken Blanchard (MJF Books, 2005), sought to establish a more biblical beachhead upon Greenleaf's foundational writings. Blanchard certainly caught the fancy of corporate thought leaders. But since then, secular media like the *Harvard Business Review* have referred to servant leadership without any mention of Jesus.

Today—especially in the marketplace—servant leadership is little more than a synonym for humility. If you're humble, you're a servant leader (so it goes); if you serve your people, you're part of the humble nobility.

Humbly serving is not a bad thing.

It's just incomplete.

## Enter the Strong Servant

Do any of the following desires resonate with you?

- "I want to be a biblical leader, but I need some fresh inspiration."
- "People often view my servanthood as weakness; I want to come across as more confident."
- "I want to serve, but I need to get people's respect first."

These sentiments echo through the board rooms of businesses, churches, governments, NGOs, and universities. If you feel the need to build authority and strength before trying out servanthood, you're not alone. It takes grit and confidence to be a humble servant.

Servant leadership is enabled by authority. But can we really command authority while we serve people? Is it possible to wield power and exhibit servanthood at the same time?

It is a strange coupling indeed.

## My Own Journey

I needed to read this book as much as I needed to write it.

For many years, I struggled to lead in a difficult environment (which is where I got the title for my book, *Leading from the Lions' Den*). My colleagues seemed to thrive on conflict. I sure didn't.

I tried to lead like a servant but couldn't compete with their charisma and intensity. How do you lead when the culture rewards ego and power?

Things changed. I became CEO a few years ago. Several people left, and new A-players came on board.

I knew I needed to up my leadership quotient. I turned back to the Bible. Since I've used it as a leadership textbook before, I resolved to take a deeper look.

This time, instead of mining just one leadership verse from each of the sixty-six books, I marked every verse throughout the entire Bible that had to do with leadership. After a while, the Holy Spirit guided me toward a vision for this book you now hold: **to call servant-minded leaders to boldly champion God's will for their companies, churches, organizations, and families.**

As I read the Bible, I was flooded by truths, concepts, and stories that renewed my passion for God's Word and for leadership. The more I read, the more I believed the Bible needed a fresh introduction into the servant leadership conversation.

## How to Use This Book

My hope for this book was to create a practical how-to tool for Christian leadership development. You'll see I've injected micro-devotions throughout the chapters, offering compact concepts and verses you can study, share, and discuss. For example:

> "God has not given us a spirit of timidity, but of power, love & self-discipline" (2 Tim. 1:7, NLT). 3 top #leadership qualities!

Simply go to servantleaderstrong.com to access a list of all of these shareable micro-devotions.

My prayer is that God's Word would lodge itself into your heart and mind long after my own words fade from your memory.

But the word of God continued to spread and flourish.

*—Acts 12:24*

## Ready for Your Journey?

Before we embark on this biblical expedition together, I want to pass on some encouragement:

When the godly are in authority, the people rejoice.
—*Proverbs 29:2a (NLT)*

People are happy when there is a godly leader at the helm. Talk about engaged employees!

But also notice the word *authority*. This implies more than a servant who happens to hold a title. It suggests control, strength, command, and rule. The Message translates the godly person in authority as the "person who runs things."

So there must be a lot more to servant leadership than serving.

Which is exactly what this book is about.

Let's now explore the riches and depth of the Bible and learn what it says about becoming servant-leader strong.

# Foreword

Leaders make people and places better. They move organizations from where they are to where they should be. Our world desperately craves good leadership.

Tragically, in an age when leadership is in great demand, people have a low view of most leaders. Many leaders today have become self-serving rather than others-serving. They pursue positions for their own benefit, not to edify others. Politicians hold office for decades. At the end of their tenure, they have bloated bank accounts, but their constituents' problems have only grown worse. Corporate executives collect generous stock options while using and discarding many of their employees. In recent years, there have been horrific disclosures of church ministers who fleeced their flock rather than shepherding them with love and integrity. The world is crying out for trustworthy leaders who make their followers' lives better.

We may suspect that the Bible contains answers for society's problems. Yet, too often we go to the Bible for trite devotional thoughts and to the world for down-to-earth leadership wisdom. While we admire Jesus and His disciples, their leadership style often appears obsolete or impractical for our modern challenges. After all, most of them died as martyrs! Modern leaders do not generally aspire to such a goal.

Misunderstandings often arise when discussing "servant leadership." Jesus is typically portrayed as humbly washing His disciples' feet and dying for them. Such leadership is inspiring during a church service but seems highly ineffective for corporate America. Yet such a view grossly misunderstands both Jesus and servant leadership. Jesus may have served His followers, but He was always their leader. His vision, authority, and influence were unparalleled. Jesus was not merely a servant; He was a servant *leader*.

As a result of Jesus's leadership, the small band of followers He led for three years grew into a worldwide movement. Two thousand years later, Jesus's followers continue to lay down their lives for Him. He has inspired much of the world's greatest art and thought. Today, despite its apparent problems, no organization on earth matches the Church's breadth, scope, diversity, and influence. Surely, Jesus was onto something!

I am so pleased with Tom Harper's book. *Servant Leader Strong* takes an insightful, thought-provoking look at Jesus's practical and effective leadership. Many authors have tackled this subject before. But this book is special. Tom is a leader who understands leadership. Better yet, he knows biblical, servant leadership. And he is an engaging communicator. This book is easy to read and difficult to put down.

Why yet another book on leadership? Because we still don't get it. We must keep learning and growing as leaders until we are leading our families, churches, businesses, and institutions the way God intended. There is too much at stake to continue leading as we always have. This book will help you move your leadership to a higher level. So read it carefully, thoughtfully, and personally. Then go out and change your world for the better.

Richard Blackaby, PhD
President of Blackaby Ministries International
and coauthor of *Spiritual Leadership* and *Experiencing God*

# Introduction:
# This Thing Called
# Servant Leadership

> " 'Do not I fill heaven and earth?' declares the Lord"
> (Jer. 23:24). Our #leadership is incomplete without a
> concept of God.

The world sees leadership as if through a veil. Without God in the picture, it ignores the effects of sin, the workings of Satan, the influence of the Holy Spirit, the wisdom of the Word, the sanctification of believers through hardship, and the eternal effects of temporal decisions. It also ignores the fact that there is a sovereign Lord, "the great King over all the earth" (Ps. 47:2).

> "What is seen is temporary, but what is unseen is eternal" (2. Cor. 4:18). #Leadership focuses on the unseen.

Though he is unseen, he exerts his will over the affairs of people and nations. The generations are vaguely aware of his workings: "The LORD reigns forever, your God, O Zion, for all generations" (Ps. 146:10). He sweeps through history, establishing kingdoms, felling rulers, and calling people to him.

God's invisibility is a mystery. It's as if he wanted it to be easy *not* to believe in him. And yet, if you have "eyes to see," he is everywhere. He is so deep and unfathomable that he must be perceived spiritually. He reveals himself through love, conviction of sin, and in the very fabric of nature. He speaks in numerous ways to those who have "ears to hear."

How far have you invited this God into your life? How far into your leadership? My prayer is that after you read this book, you will desire more of him in your everyday work, whether you lead a team of three or a company of 30,000.

I hope to show you that he is reliable, not just for salvation and the deep spiritual things of life, but also that he says volumes about how he wants you to lead the people around you. The good news is that he promises to walk with you, guide you, protect you, sharpen you, and be your personal confidant.

I believe a big part of servant leadership is "strength under control." As the perfect servant leader, Jesus exhibited restrained power during his life on earth, but he didn't start that way. He started life as a weak, helpless baby, like the rest of us.

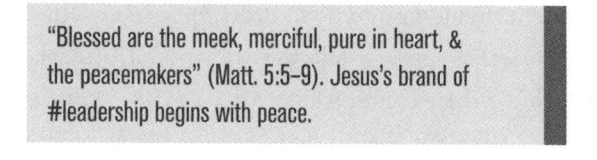

"Blessed are the meek, merciful, pure in heart, & the peacemakers" (Matt. 5:5–9). Jesus's brand of #leadership begins with peace.

While he began in peace, he also displayed a brilliant style of authoritative leadership that commanded respect and stirred up thousands of followers willing to die for him.

And though we likely won't attract such steadfast servants ourselves, he still makes an incredible promise: "[W]hoever believes in me will do the works I have been doing, and they will do even greater things than these" (John 14:12).

So, our work is cut out for us. That's what Paul the "super apostle" understood when he wrote this:

"I worked harder than all of them—yet not I, but the grace of God that was with me" (1 Cor. 15:10). True #leadership is GOD working.

Paul revealed the power behind his great accomplishments, a power at our disposal too—"the grace of God with me."

This is servant leadership. Full of grace and peace, power and authority.

## Aligning Our Concept of Leadership

We see that godly leadership is more than discovering what the organization should be and do in order to be successful. It's also more than setting up our followers to succeed (though it certainly includes these concepts).

Godly leadership begins, flourishes, and grows over time as the leader develops character, good followers, wisdom, and most importantly, a strong walk with the Holy Spirit.

Now, with our foundation built, let's begin in an uncomfortable place.

## PART I

# Standing Strong:
# How to Overcome Internal
# and External Resistance

# CHAPTER 1

# Sin

## Introduction

> "The heart is deceitful above all things and
> beyond cure."
>
> —*Jeremiah 17:9a*

Despite what the average non-Christian believes, people are not inherently good. The Bible makes this clear throughout. We are sinners not just in word, deed, or thought, but in our very nature.

Because of this nature, we can't help but sin. We may sin less when the Holy Spirit lives inside us, but I believe even the most devout Christians will be surprised when they enter heaven and look back on their earthly existence. We will likely recoil at the thousands of "little" sins we committed and thought nothing of.

There are many leadership killers, but sin is the most insidious. It wages war on us from all sides. It launches small detachments to harass us while its artillery moves into position for a full-on assault. Just when we think we've beaten it, another snarling head rises from the shadows.

Too many leaders have fallen because of personal sin. Bad character, overweening pride, lying, adultery—you know the list. If we feel confident we're out of the clear and let down our guard, it's at that moment Satan will strike.

Therefore, we must build strong walls of defense. The Word exhorts us to anticipate our enemy, to post vigilant watch at every outpost in our life and work. God also gives us his Word to fight back against attacks and temptations.

> "Sin desires to have you, but you must master it" (Gen. 4:7). Sin doesn't control us.

If we want to lead as servants, we must resist this taskmaster. For when sin rules over a leader, his or her followers are vulnerable as well.

Ironically, our true Master is inside us, right where our deepest sins reside.

> "Forgive my hidden faults. Keep me also from willful sins" (Ps 19:12-13). #Leadership starts inside with God.

Our never-ending battle with sin is most intense in the unseen self. Let's examine how sin can eat away at our inner lives before breaking through to the sunlight.

## The Worst Kind of Leadership Sin

What lurks inside the leader? Only lust, stress, fatigue, pride, impatience, bitterness, jealousy. It's dark in there.

Most sin can be hidden from the outside world. But when the secrets aren't confessed to the Lord, they fester, grow, deepen, and threaten to emerge.

They're dangerous when they meet the light. Consider a married pastor who hid an affair with his female executive pastor for several years. People in the church couldn't put their finger on the reasons, but the congregation had stopped growing and suffered division. You can imagine the complete devastation when the affair became public.

How can this kind of thing happen?

> [B]ut each person is tempted when they are dragged away by their own evil desire and enticed. Then, after desire has conceived, it gives birth to sin; and sin, when it is full-grown, gives birth to death. (Jas. 1:14–15)

The pastor's secret sexual sin had burned away his conscience. After getting away with it for so many years, he didn't feel the need to repent and flee from it.

Unconfessed, rotting sin has many consequences:

- It removes God's hand of blessing.
- It creates a spirit of discord, pride, and negativity.
- It destroys marriages.
- People sense it.
- It gives the enemy a foothold and opens the leader to attack.
- The leader's family and the flock under his care become vulnerable.

There's an even greater danger for him personally: judgment.

> "God will judge men's secrets through Jesus Christ" (Rom. 2:16). Secret sins not only ruin #leadership, they are seen by God NOW.

Is there an unseen sin in your own life? If you can't think of one, praise the Lord. If you're not sure, ask the Holy Spirit to reveal a sin guilt the enemy may be using against you. Satan likes to remind us of our past, but repentance breaks his power.

If the Spirit leads you to seek forgiveness, it may be painful, but the freedom is healing and life-giving.

> "We have sinned. . . . Please rescue us. . . He could bear Israel's misery no longer" (Judg. 10:15-16). Repentance moves God. #leadership

## Willfully Lead Yourself Away from Sin

> "I find this law at work: Although I want to do good, evil is right there with me" (Rom. 7:21). Sin creeps into even the best #leadership.

Our will is weak. Even when we want to obey, Jesus said, "The spirit is willing, but the flesh is weak" (Matt. 26:41). C. S. Lewis wrote in *Mere Christianity*, "No man knows how bad he is till he has tried very hard to be good."

Despite this sobering fact, there are still things we can do when it comes to fighting sin—or rather, things to *not* do. Here are seven.

1. Don't look at things you shouldn't.

> "I will set before my eyes no vile thing" (Ps 101:3). #Leadership begins with self-discipline.

2.  Don't let your anger control you.

> "In your anger do not sin" (Ps. 4:4). Even the most passionate #leadership must have self-control.

3.  Deny yourself physically.

> We have power over sin; "therefore do not let sin reign in your body so that you obey its desires" (Rom. 6:12).

4.  Don't think about how to satisfy sinful desires.

> "Do not think about how to gratify the desires of the sinful nature" (Rom. 13:14). #Leadership power can feed these desires.

5.  Don't think you're exempt because you're a leader.

> "Jesus came into the world to save sinners—of whom I am the worst" (1 Tim. 1:15). #Leadership recognizes what the self lacks.

6. Don't sin just because others do.

> "Do not imitate what is evil but what is good" (3 John 11). #Leadership is vulnerable to culture. We must resist.

7. Don't set yourself up for future regret.

> "What benefit did you reap at that time from the things you are now ashamed of? Those things result in death!" (Rom. 6:21).

To put a period on the don't-do theme in this chapter, let's not forget the cardinal sin of omission:

> Anyone, then, who knows the good he ought to do and doesn't do it, sins. (Jas. 4:17)

In other words, when you have a chance to do something you know is good, take that chance! God gives us the ability to choose good or evil in virtually every waking moment.

This choice is the essence of leading ourselves—and a prerequisite for leading others.

## Fight Sin with Fear

> "God has come to test you, so that the fear of God will be with you to keep you from sinning" (Exod. 20:20). Godly #leadership is tested.

There are many kinds of fear associated with sin. Here are a few.

- Fear of being found out
- Fear of punishment
- Fear of hurting others
- Fear of damaging your fellowship with God
- Fear of bringing disrepute to God's name

In his mercy, God allows these fears into our hearts to help us repent from sin and turn from it. If we do, he is glorified, our relationship with him is restored, and the enemy loses his foothold in our lives.

The Lord desires our fear because he loves us and doesn't want us to sin. The natural consequences of sin aren't always enough to deter us or to drive us to seek forgiveness.

Think about someone you love dearly. Are you afraid of hurting them? Why? If you knew they would forgive you eventually and love you no matter what, why does it still bother you to hurt them?

We're afraid of hurting those we love because it will cause them pain. They'll be sad. They may be confused about who we really are, that maybe they made a mistake when they let us into their heart in an intimate way.

> Wanna not sin? "Through the fear of the Lord a man avoids evil" (Prov. 16:6). #leadership

## Manage the Sin Around You

As a leader, dealing with sin in others is every bit as difficult and frustrating as fighting our own.

Perhaps the best way to handle this sin, other than with wisdom and grace, is to understand it is the root of most people problems in an organization.

Just look around:

> "The acts of the flesh are obvious: sexual immorality, impurity and debauchery; idolatry and witchcraft; hatred, discord, jealousy, fits of rage, selfish ambition, dissensions, factions and envy . . ." (Gal. 5:19–21a)

Lest we think we're above these "obvious" sins, listen to Paul the Apostle's admission:

> "What I want to do I do not do, but what I hate I do" (Rom. 7:15). Why we will always have people problems!

It's sad, true, and unavoidable. We ourselves are sinful beyond measure, as are all our coworkers, family members, and friends.

But there's good news and a charge for all Christian leaders:

> "While we were still sinners, Christ died for us" (Rom. 5:8). With such love shown me, my #leadership must reflect it to others.

With the world's sin never more prevalent or accepted, may the Lord bless your leadership in these dark times.

## Fight Sin with Love

> "Love each other deeply, because love covers over a multitude of sins" (1 Pet. 4:8). #Leadership is not exempt from this activity.

Jesus' act of sacrifice was ultimate love; however, it was anything but warm and fuzzy. It was grisly and dark. Painful and bloody.

His love was so powerful that for our sake he willingly submitted to the tidal wave of sin that rolled over him. He had never known sin within his own heart, yet the Father allowed him to be crushed by it.

As horrifying as it must have been to experience this taste of hell and separation from God, our Lord completely surrendered himself to it. He knew he would die a horrible death both physically and spiritually. Yet he also knew he would live again and be glorified in victory over sin, death, and Satan!

As 1 Peter 4:8 says, the love of God through Jesus covered over a multitude of sins—the whole world's. Jesus himself told his disciples, "Greater love has no one than this: to lay down one's life for one's friends" (John 15:13).

Love is a powerful force most leaders leave in their back pockets. We can show "leadership love" by being patient, merciful, sacrificing, and forgiving. I'm not advocating sweeping people's wrongs under the carpet; rather, we should filter our knee-jerk reactions through love.

> "But he who has been forgiven little loves little" (Luke 7:47). Concerned with org #culture? Mercy increases love!

A culture of love is an employee's ultimate working environment. When they feel a sense of dignity, when their leaders seek to understand before they berate or blame, when the staff feels cared for, organizational culture blossoms.

Mercy triumphs over judgment. (Jas. 2:13)

## CHAPTER 2

# Motivation

## Introduction

> "Tell Archippus: 'See to it that you complete the ministry you have received in the Lord'" (Col. 4:17). Press on! #leadership

Motivation is fickle and intensely personal. On Twitter's #leadership stream a minute ago, I saw someone post, "Get up and start your day with enthusiasm. Enthusiasm breeds enthusiasm!"

Then I looked in on my "close follows" list and saw an author friend's post: "It's never too late to be what you might have been."

Which quote motivates you more? Does it depend on the day or hour whether you need a dose of passion versus the freedom to dream?

I'm revved by vision. God made me a dreamer, which totally conflicted with my wife's practical nature when we first met. She tolerated my visions of grandeur for a while, until I started acting on them. They became more than daydreams and most definitely did not pay the bills right away.

Some of us are motivated by rewards and money, others by meaningful work. Some get inspired by being around people, others by being alone.

A former colleague of mine was Mr. Enthusiasm. He was one of the best salespeople I've ever known. He was so full of passion and energy that you couldn't be around him without feeling a lift.

Some people go to conferences and come home with a buzz of ideas and excitement. But often the glow fades and they revert to ho-humness, never acting on the momentary energy. Others read books, highlighting all the great ideas, but then the tome goes on their shelf, replaced by a new one.

Hunger and fear are effective motivators. So is jealousy.

> "All labor & all achievement spring from man's envy of his neighbor" (Eccl. 4:4). #Leadership can't alter our sin nature; only God can.

Motivation is smoke, seldom remaining consistent, gone in an instant. And overshadowed by our sinful nature.

So how, then, does a leader effectively motivate herself and others to persevere and exceed expectations?

## Five Ways to Spark Zeal

> "Never be lacking in zeal, but keep your spiritual fervor, serving the Lord" (Rom. 12:11). Spiritual zeal fuels #leadership.

How do you build your energy and maintain your daily drive? Several verses are instructive for filling our followers—and ourselves—with the ambition required to succeed in our work.

**1. Be ready for bad stuff.** The Israelite workers rebuilding the wall around Jerusalem were always ready for attacks.

> "Those who carried materials did their work with one hand & held a weapon in the other" (Neh. 4:17). #determination

In the same way, we should temper our positive attitude with the possibility that something could come along and spoil it at any time. When we're on the lookout for critics, naysayers, or setbacks, we're not completely taken off guard when a shoe does in fact drop. And when things go smoothly, our battle readiness translates into overall leadership strength.

> "Stop trusting in man, who has but a breath in his nostrils" (Isa. 2:22a). People have built-in fallibility. #leadership

I just received an attitude-spoiling email from a new business acquaintance. We'd only talked once and exchanged a few emails since our initial discussion a week earlier. In his note this afternoon, not only did he misinterpret something I'd said, but he accused me of lying and operating "in bad faith."

After I fumed at my screen, I had to laugh at the irony. Apparently, the Lord wanted to use me as an object lesson!

**2. Grow your roots.** When we immerse ourselves in God's Word, prayer, worship, and fellowship with other believers, our spiritual strength grows, increasing our joy and energy as a result.

> "Your roots will grow down into God's love and keep you strong" (Eph. 3:17, NLT).

**3. Pay attention to your physical needs.** Sometimes it's as simple as eating, sleeping, exercising, or just refraining from regular work.

> Worn out by #leadership? So was Elijah. " 'I've had enough, Lord,' he said. . . . An angel said, 'Get up & eat.' " (1 Kgs. 19:4–5). Good advice!

> "Jesus to his leaders: 'Come with me by yourselves to a quiet place and get some rest' " (Mark 6:31).

**4. Fulfill desires.** You know what it's like to reach a lofty goal. Can you help others experience the same rush of accomplishment?

> "A longing fulfilled is sweet to the soul" (Prov. 13:19). Why #leadership should help people achieve dreams.

**5. Remember who your real boss is.** Sometimes we need to look past our earthly superiors at the King who watches our every move. It is he who will ultimately judge our work. He will fulfill his purposes through what we do on earth. When we seek his guidance and his strength—and we're willing to follow his lead—our zeal for the task at hand will be refreshed.

> "Whatever you do, whether in word or deed, do it all in the name of the Lord Jesus" (Col. 3:17). Daily #leadership reminder.

## The Most Powerful Motivator for Leaders

A few words from the prophet Azariah motivated King Asa of Judah to up his leadership performance. The same exhortation can motivate anyone in leadership today too.

The prophet simply told the king to look beyond the vision he had for his kingdom. Beyond the history of accomplishments, current circumstances, and daily grind.

He said, "Be strong and do not give up, for your work will be rewarded" (2 Chron. 15:7).

In so many words, Azariah told the king to look forward to the divine reward that would follow a life of perseverance.

The promise of future rewards motivates many leaders. It does me. When we pour into people's lives, drip our sweat and blood into a business, sacrifice financially to start a church, or give time and treasure to causes that matter to us, it's incredibly encouraging to know God's watching and will reward us.

Is that self-centered? No, it's biblical. I'll illustrate with two verses:

[Moses] regarded disgrace for the sake of Christ as of greater value than the treasures of Egypt, because he was looking ahead to his reward. (Heb. 11:26)

Look, I am coming soon! My reward is with me, and I will give to each person according to what they have done. (Rev. 22:12)

Are you looking beyond your leadership vision to the day when Christ will smile as he bestows your reward?

Vision statements are good motivators, but God's promised rewards truly inspire.

## Faithfully Evaluate the Future

"Many are the plans in a man's heart, but it's the Lord's purpose that prevails (Prov. 19:21). Planning is good, but remember whose plan you'll follow.

When we wait on the Lord to accomplish something, we know that if and when he decides to do it, the timing will be perfect. All the right dependencies will have happened so that his overarching plan—of which we are a part—plays out according to his will.

Sometimes I wonder if I'm doing enough to grow our company. Am I wasting time on this project or that? Do I need to be bolder? Do I need to work harder? Do I need to risk more? Do I need to pull back and let my key leaders do their jobs?

Every leader asks self-critical questions like these. Some answers are obvious. Others come only in hindsight.

But even then, we won't see God's complete purposes and plan. He wants us to trust him along the way, all the way till the end.

This is faithful, future-oriented leadership.

> "Why, you do not even know what will happen tomorrow" (Jas. 4:14a). Strategic planning needs to have a loose grip.

## Plan with an Open Hand

> There is no wisdom, no insight, no plan
> that can succeed against the LORD.
> —*Proverbs 21:30*

I used to spend so much time planning for the year ahead, budgeting, and goal-committing—but the years have shown me that such precise planning is a waste of time.

Some of the work helped, but things never happened just as we laid them out. We produced so many reports, pro formas, and forecasts that many of our revenue-producing projects were put on hold for weeks. And of course the delay made it that much harder to achieve the sales goals we'd spent so much time setting!

Budgeting is a necessity—we are of course to count the cost before doing the work. But just when we think the future is in hand, the Lord reminds us he's the one in control. Life changes, the markets spins sideways, people come and go.

When plans seem perfect or our vision casts an exciting future, we must hold on to them loosely. God's authority and power overshadow them.

> "The Lord foils the plans of the nations; he thwarts the purposes of the peoples" (Ps. 33:10). God's mysterious #leadership.

God is mysterious indeed. He wants us to plan, yet he changes those plans.

> "A man's steps are directed by the Lord. How then can anyone understand his own way?" (Prov. 20:24) #Leadership accepts the mystery.

In light of God's higher plans, what are we to do? We pray for his will to be revealed, to conform us to his will, to inspire our thinking, to direct our steps.

Sometimes he confirms his guidance with striking clarity.

> "The reason the dream was given to Pharaoh in 2 forms is that the matter has been firmly decided by God . . ." (Gen. 41:32). God affirms his direction.

I have a friend who leads a vibrant ministry, but he has also suffered much (including the early death of his beloved wife, who also was his ministry partner).

He told me this morning during a strategy meeting that he doesn't have the fire like he did ten years ago with regard to growing the ministry and launching new projects. These days he leads with more of an open hand, grabbing onto what God brings his way. He waits for confirmation and doesn't overreact to redirection.

I was humbled as I thought about the work I do for God. How much of it is personal ambition versus divine direction? Hard one to answer.

Lord, hold my hand open and fill it with the fruit of *your* plan.

> "This is to my Father's glory, that you bear much fruit, showing yourself to be my disciples" (John 15:8). Is your #leadership fruitful?

## Get After Life

> "All the days ordained 4 me were written in your book before 1 of them came to be" (Ps. 139:16). God isn't surprised. #leadership

Francine, a long-time friend of our family, is in the last days of her life. She has been an inspiration to us because in the midst of her devastating cancer, she can't stop talking about where she's going.

Francine's like a child on the way to Disney World. She smiles through her pain. She can't get out of bed anymore, but her eyes dance with excitement.

The Bible wants us to look at the future with such anticipation. Though we may not see an end to difficulties, the finish line is approaching, and an exciting destination awaits.

As we lead, let's look beyond our mission and even our longest-term vision. God wants us to grapple with our daily challenges with forever firmly in view.

> "He determined the times set for them & the exact places where they should live" (Acts 17:26). God put us in #leadership right here, right now.

How we lead and live matters during the days God has given us. Our future—even into eternity—depends on decisions we make in the present.

Life really is short. Let's get after it!

> As you lead, run. "Run in such a way as to get the prize" (1 Cor. 9:24). #leadership

## A Prayer for the Imposter in Your Chair

> [May God] equip you with everything good for doing his will, and may he work in us what is pleasing to him, through Jesus Christ, to whom be glory for ever and ever. Amen.
>
> —*Hebrews 13:21*

Do you ever feel weak or inadequate in your position of authority? I don't mean when you're in your afternoon slump or just having a down day, but rather those times when you feel insufficient in general.

Some call it the "imposter complex," when the leader hopes no one finds out he or she isn't cut out for the job.

Hebrews 13:21 is a great prayer to recite when we feel like this. It's a prayer God will answer because he gives it to us in his Word. Not only will he equip us to do the work he wants us to do, he will change us in ways that please him.

"Lord," you could say, "I'm not good enough to do this job you've called me to do. Equip me, change me, show me what your will is. You've promised to do this through the power of Jesus Christ who lived and died so that I could be yours. Amen."

He will swap your inadequacy with his infinite power, which the writer of Hebrews describes in verse 20 as a power that "brought back from the dead our Lord Jesus."

If God has dominion over life and death, imagine what he could do with your leadership.

## Let Hunger Motivate

The Bible teaches that the most basic motivational force is something we all possess: hunger.

> The laborer's appetite works for him; his hunger drives him on. (Prov. 16:26)

Motivation is intrinsic; whatever we hunger for works for us. It compels us to work to satisfy it.

Certainly this fits the literal meaning for food. Second Thessalonians 3:10 says, "The one who is unwilling to work shall not eat."

But we also hunger for other things. Recognition. Money. Relationships. Accomplishment. We want to prove ourselves. We want to leave a legacy.

And then there are negative motivators, like fear, embarrassment, financial emergencies, or one-upping the neighbors.

Any of these things motivates us at different times in our lives, even at different times of the day.

Motivation is not something a leader can lasso. It's a personal force akin to the hunger of a laborer.

The leader can simply let whatever hunger a worker is feeling do its work. And give him or her solid leadership as they drive themselves forward.

## Bored or Down? Try This

Many leaders begin their careers or new jobs with a great surge of energy, excitement, and anticipation. But what do you do when the energy starts to wane?

Let me give you an idea that has rejuvenated me and other leaders I know:

**Start leading differently.**

Sounds simple, but I mean it literally: lead differently than you did yesterday, last month, or last year.

Here's an example. It's common knowledge that as a church or business grows, the leader is supposed to delegate more and do less. But why wait for that new level of growth? Delegate something that's eaten you up for the past month and see if you don't brighten.

Already a super delegator? Try taking a person, project, or product under your wing. Micromanage something that interests you.

A change-up in either direction could energize you and give you a reason to look forward to getting up tomorrow.

Leading differently could mean more self-focus and getting more sleep or exercise. Take some time off to write or build something. Read a good book. (Novels are OK.)

Serve someone. Share the gospel. Have coffee with an encouraging friend. Schedule solitude into your day.

I feel better when I accomplish tasks, achieve small wins, or connect with my people. The energy pick-up spurs me on to the next person or task, and the momentum builds.

Tried all that and still feel empty? Thank God for your job and make a list of things you love about it. Let him shift your perspective in the process.

Maybe leading differently for you is simply following him more closely.

"... he leads me beside quiet waters, he refreshes my soul" (Ps. 23:2b–3a).

## CHAPTER 3

# Fear, Worry, and Facing the Impossible

## Introduction

What are you most afraid of in life? I believe there are four main categories that describe our fears and worries:

- **Emotional**: Some of us are deathly afraid of being left out, left behind, left unprotected, or left altogether. The woman whose husband deserted her or the son who finds himself orphaned as a teenager deal with feelings of abandonment and vulnerability. Even the fear of public speaking can rattle our emotions and drive us to escape any situation that promises unwanted attention.
- **Physical**: We're all afraid of the threat of pain, whether of heights, fire, planes, drowning, dogs, intruders, or whatever else in life can harm us.

- **Financial**: We can stress about providing for our families, an inability to pay bills, an insecure future, job loss, creditors, letters from the IRS, or catastrophic loss.
- **Spiritual**: Many people fear the unseen spiritual realm. Plus, if they're afraid of death and an unknowable eternity, they often consciously avoid thinking about them altogether or default to the other extreme: unbiblical obsession with them.

This section explores an overview of the Bible's prescriptions for fear and worry, and ends with the one fear that will save us from all the rest.

## Desperately Pursue God's Peace

Have you ever woken up with a sudden realization that your company could fall apart at any moment? I've had this feeling several times over the years.

Perhaps the enemy brings these fears to mind. Sometimes tiredness or stress intensifies them. Whatever the source, there's a common starting point for all believers in our battle against worry, stress, fear, and spiritual oppression.

> "Cast your cares on the Lord and he will sustain you" (Ps. 55:22). #Leadership is not solo.

"Cast all your anxiety on him because he cares for you" (1 Pet. 5:7). The best stress management! #leadership

In the Old Testament, an army of Israelite tribes feared imminent defeat. They cried out to God in the midst of the battle crushing in around them. Can you guess what happened next?

"He answered their prayers, because they trusted in him" (1 Chron. 5:20). Desperation + trust = God's victory. #leadership

God of course won't dispatch every enemy we face in such miraculous fashion. Sometimes we just have to keep fighting. This is what perseverance is all about.

But again, we have clear instructions from on high:

"Don't worry about anything; instead, pray about everything. Tell God what you need." (Phil. 4:6, NLT). Formula for worry-free #leadership.

A great promise is revealed in the next verse: "Then you will experience God's peace . . ." The Message adds new color in its translation: "Before you know it, a sense of God's wholeness, everything coming together for good, will come and settle you down."

God's peace is powerful. While it may not come easily, the Lord wants us to fall down in desperate, trusting prayer as we cry out for it.

## Raise the Shield

> "Our struggle is not against flesh & blood" (Eph. 6:12). Biblical #leadership realizes who is really against us.

I had planned to write this section for a long time and unintentionally got to it tonight. As God would have it, an intense spiritual battle ripped through my family this afternoon, and when I opened the manuscript this evening to work on it, the timing was a little eerie.

I suppose the Lord allowed today's events to happen to refresh my memory about how real the enemy is. Satan really does prowl around looking for someone to devour (1 Pet. 5:8). His demonic forces wait for the right moment to strike. But God uses even the devil's own tactics for our ultimate good (see Rom. 8:28).

And so here I am, fresh from the battlefield, marveling at the power of Jesus's name. Worshipping him as the One who not only delivered my family today, but who defeated our common enemy so many centuries ago.

For some reason, that enemy is still allowed to operate. Sinful human nature invites his companionship, empowering him to cast his net far and wide. If we manage to evade it, his arrows still seek us. But even against those we have a remedy:

> "The shield of faith . . . can extinguish all the flaming arrows of the evil one" (Eph. 6:16). Promise for dark times in our #leadership.

God built up my faith today; his shield was strong. Sometimes painful spiritual attacks end up strengthening us as believers. When we emerge from them with the armor of God in place, we're equipped to help others with their own battles.

Paul illustrates this concept beautifully:

> "As you know, it was because of an illness that I first preached the gospel to you" (Gal. 4:13). Opportunity out of hardship!

If it weren't for Paul's personal suffering, certain people wouldn't have heard the gospel and responded the way they did. I pray my own battle today encourages you and enforces the gospel in your life.

## When You Face the Impossible

The angel Gabriel told two unlikely women they were about to conceive. The problem was Elizabeth was well past child-bearing years, and Mary was an unmarried virgin.

The two NIV translations (1984 and 2011) render Gabriel's words in Luke 1:37 in complementary ways:

"For nothing is impossible with God." (1984 NIV)

"For no word from God will ever fail." (2011 NIV)

When God works or speaks, he accomplishes the impossible. He delivered on his promise to the women, not just for their own happiness, but for the good of mankind. (The two children would be John the Baptist and Jesus.)

This leads to a few questions to ponder:

1. What "impossible" challenge are you facing right now?
2. What is God trying to accomplish in you through this thing?
3. What might he be accomplishing for the good of others?
4. How will a victory bring glory to God?

The answers to questions two through four should guide you on how to lean in and rely on God's leading.

> "God is our God for ever and ever; he will be our
> guide even to the end" (Ps. 48:14). Guide me, Lord.
> #leadership

## Fear the Lord; Don't Be Afraid

One of the great paradoxes in Scripture is the fear of the Lord.
It's confusing because he tells us to fear him, yet he then seeks to
dispel our fears.

Jesus clears up this conundrum in the book of Luke. He
gave his disciples a private lesson before releasing them to corral
the masses crowding in to be healed and fed and taught.

### 1. Fear God because he alone can send people to heaven or hell.

It may not be popular to say that the Lord sends people to eternal punishment, but it's hard to dispute Jesus's own teaching on
the matter:

> I tell you, my friends, do not be afraid of those who
> kill the body and after that can do no more. But I will
> show you whom you should fear: Fear him who, after
> your body has been killed, has authority to throw
> you into hell. Yes, I tell you, fear him. (Luke 12:4–5)

Who would want to worship a God that sends people to hell? Good question. Let's hear the rest of Jesus's answer.

## 2. Don't be afraid, because God knows you, values you, and loves you beyond comprehension.

> Are not five sparrows sold for two pennies? Yet not one of them is forgotten by God. Indeed, the very hairs of your head are all numbered. Don't be afraid; you are worth more than many sparrows." (Luke 12:6–7)

The picture Jesus paints here is one of extreme intimacy. Who else in the world knows how many hairs we have? What else might he know about us that no one else—including we ourselves—could possibly fathom?

Of course he's speaking here to his disciples, most of whom believe he is the Son of God, and therefore are in a position to claim the second promise of intimacy with the Father. The masses Jesus was about to teach hadn't yet accepted (or understood) God's love.

As leaders, we must first have a healthy fear/love relationship with the Lord. Then we will understand how to wield authority.

The lesson from his passage could be a framed quote to be read by all who enter your organization:

> Fear the consequences of bad behavior, but if you truly seek forgiveness, you will be welcomed with open arms.

## CHAPTER 4

# Criticism and Opposition

## Introduction

No one likes criticism. It bites into our soft flesh, leaving a mark that takes a while to heal. Even those of us claiming to have thick skin get side-swiped every now and then.

I've watched certain leaders (especially politicians) weather it better than others, but upon closer observation, they were by nature pot-stirrers who thrived off conflict and tension. Criticism energized them because they loved a fight. Debates were like manhood-proving bar brawls.

For us mere mortals, the struggle remains.

## A Simple Way to Avoid Criticism

> "Do everything without complaining & arguing, so that no one can criticize you" (Phil. 2:14–15). #Leaders are not complainers.

So there it is. The less we complain and argue, the less we get criticized.

Negativity breeds negativity. Complaining usually means you're criticizing someone else; arguing all the time bares a critical spirit.

As the leader goes, so go the people. Critical leaders encourage critical followers. But people find it hard to criticize positive leaders.

## When Our Friends Swipe at Us

> Jesus said to them, "A prophet is not without honor except in his own town, among his relatives and in his own home."
>
> —*Mark 6:4*

Ever feel unjustly criticized by friends or family members?

I can think of two general reasons this might happen to us. First, God knows we need to be humbled, and rarely will you find someone willing to humble *themselves*. It's a job for the people who care about us the most!

After people unimpressed by who we've become put us back in our place, God wants to be the one to lift us up because in so doing, he glorifies himself.

But there's another reason:

> The person without the Spirit does not accept the things that come from the Spirit of God but considers them foolishness, and cannot understand them because they are discerned only through the Spirit. (1 Cor. 2:14)

The unbelieving people close to us need grace because they don't understand the things of God. They don't know how God works through humility and servanthood; they surely can't grasp what it means to glorify him.

Therefore, let's not judge them for their lack of faith and worldly ways. Let's just keep moving, like Jesus did. "He did not do many miracles [in his hometown] because of their lack of faith" (Matt. 13:58).

When we feel discouraged by those around us—for whatever reason—shouldn't we look upward for encouragement?

> "Surely God is my help; the Lord is the one who sustains me" (Ps. 54:4). When we don't feel the love in #leadership.

## Understand Satan's Role in God's Refining Process

Satan loves to fling accusations and condemnations at godly leaders. Recently a good friend of mine was nominated to a high-visibility board in the community, but because he had publicly spoken biblical truth in the past, the local media said he was unfit for the position.

Which couldn't be further from the truth—my friend had launched and sold successful businesses, started a venture capital group, even entertained going into politics at one time. For years he was an outstanding leader in the city and in church. He was more than qualified for this role!

But since "the god of this age has blinded the minds of unbelievers" (2 Cor. 4:4), the liberal media won the day and my friend turned down the position.

> "Satan rose up against Israel & incited David to take a census" (1 Chron. 21:1). Even David's #leadership was attacked. Get ready.

I learned that no matter who you are, you are a target of Satan. He waits for the smallest opening, then stretches it into a portal if he can and walks through.

I also learned through this leader's humility and mature response that God allows us to be humbled for his own reasons. He doesn't waste hardships when it comes to our refinement and sanctification.

> Until the time came to fulfill his dreams, the LORD tested Joseph's character (Ps. 105:19, NLT).

"Some time later God tested Abraham" (Gen. 22:1). Even an accomplished leader gets prepared for the next level.

Success never guarantees immunity. Not even decades of community service and public accolades mean you'll be free of ridicule from the very community you've served.

And if you're a younger leader, there may be a defining, refining moment coming your way, as modeled by Christ:

"Jesus was led by the Spirit into the wilderness to be tempted by the devil" (Matt. 4:1). Jesus' own #leadership began with difficulty.

## When Threatened, Remember Nehemiah 4

"But we prayed to our God & posted a guard" (Neh. 4:9). Meet #leadership challenges with prayer AND action.

Most of us won't lead in wartime or be attacked by malicious competitors or stockholders, but people who lead effectively in such situations have much to teach about facing opposition.

Nehemiah is one of the starkest examples of this in the Bible. Chapter 4 of his book is a valuable study of a spiritual response to strong opposition. Let's walk through a homiletic of this amazing story.

### The Initial Threat

<sup>1</sup> When Sanballat heard that we were rebuilding the wall, he became angry and was greatly incensed. He ridiculed the Jews, <sup>2</sup> and in the presence of his associates and the army of Samaria, he said, **"What are those feeble Jews doing? Will they restore their wall? . . ."**

<sup>3</sup> Tobiah the Ammonite, who was at his side, said, "What they are building—even a fox climbing up on it would break down their wall of stones!"

### Nehemiah's First Response: Prayer

[4] Hear us, our God, for we are despised. **Turn their insults back on their own heads.** Give them over as plunder in a land of captivity. [5] Do not cover up their guilt or blot out their sins from your sight, for they have thrown insults in the face of the builders.

### Then, Action

[6] **So we rebuilt the wall** till all of it reached half its height, for the people worked with all their heart.

### The Threat Intensifies

[7] But when Sanballat, Tobiah, the Arabs, the Ammonites and the people of Ashdod heard that the repairs to Jerusalem's walls had gone ahead and that the gaps were being closed, they were very angry. [8] **They all plotted together to come and fight against Jerusalem** and stir up trouble against it.

### Nehemiah Prays and Acts Again

[9] **But we prayed** to our God **and posted a guard** day and night to meet this threat.

## But It's Not Enough

<sup>10</sup> Meanwhile, the people in Judah said, "The strength of the laborers is giving out, and there is so much rubble that **we cannot rebuild the wall**."

<sup>11</sup> Also our enemies said, "Before they know it or see us, we will be right there among them and will kill them and put an end to the work."

<sup>12</sup> Then the Jews who lived near them came and told us ten times over, "**Wherever you turn, they will attack us**."

## So He Encourages His People

<sup>13</sup> Therefore I stationed some of the people behind the lowest points of the wall at the exposed places, posting them by families, with their swords, spears and bows. <sup>14</sup> After I looked things over, I stood up and said to the nobles, the officials and the rest of the people, "**Don't be afraid of them. Remember the Lord, who is great and awesome, and fight** for your families, your sons and your daughters, your wives and your homes."

¹⁵ When our enemies heard that we were aware of their plot and that God had frustrated it, we all returned to the wall, each to our own work.

## Then He Gets Strategic

¹⁶ From that day on, half of my men did the work, while the other half were equipped with spears, shields, bows and armor. The officers posted themselves behind all the people of Judah ¹⁷ who were building the wall. **Those who carried materials did their work with one hand and held a weapon in the other,** ¹⁸ **and each of the builders wore his sword at his side as he worked.** But the man who sounded the trumpet stayed with me.

¹⁹ Then I said to the nobles, the officials and the rest of the people, "The work is extensive and spread out, and we are widely separated from each other along the wall. ²⁰ Wherever you hear the sound of the trumpet, join us there. Our God will fight for us!"

²¹ So we continued the work with half the men holding spears, from the first light of dawn till the stars came out. ²² At that time I also said to the people,

"Have every man and his helper stay inside Jerusalem at night, so they can serve us as guards by night and as workers by day." [23] Neither I nor my brothers nor my men nor the guards with me took off our clothes; each had his weapon, even when he went for water.

After further intimidation, political pressure, assassination attempts, and lies, the climax to the story comes in chapter 6. Nehemiah continues his disciplined prayer and wise actions, and we finally get to the end:

[15] So **the wall was completed** on the twenty-fifth of Elul, in fifty-two days.

[16] When all our enemies heard about this, all the surrounding nations were afraid and lost their self-confidence, because they realized that this work had been done with the help of our God.

Do you see the interplay of prayer, faith, and action in this great leader? Nehemiah served his people by obeying God's direction to build the wall. But he was no pushover servant. He resisted his enemies with shows of strength and crafty strategy.

I believe Christianity is an active faith. It is intensely practical in the "real" world. When we lead like the shrewd Nehemiah, we will find "servant leadership" is virtually a misnomer.

## The Three-Step Plan to Good Anger

Jesus teaches us to love our enemies. But how do you reconcile that with his overturning of the tables in the temple? Or what about his heated debates with the Pharisees?

Should we display the same flashes of passion and anger at times?

Jesus allowed his divine anger to flare when he was defending his father's honor and rebuking liars who kept the truth from people. When it came to defending others, he stepped up.

But when people attacked him personally, he didn't resist in the typical human way. He saw it as an opportunity to love them in the midst of their sin, "for they do not know what they are doing" (Luke 23:34).

When we are personally insulted or attacked, we are to follow his example and look to the Lord to defend us. Our self-defense should be love.

But when God's name, his truth, or his children are attacked—or when the poor or needy are taken advantage of—we are to respond with Jesus's fiery defense.

How do we know the difference between our anger and that of Christ? The first step is to slow down.

> "Everyone should be quick to listen, slow to speak and slow to become angry, because human anger does not produce the righteousness that God desires." (Jas. 1:19b–20)

The second step is to seek the outcome God would desire. We can ask the Holy Spirit to give us discernment, words, and guidance. Even in the heat of the moment.

Thirdly, and most importantly, we should love. If steps one and two slip our minds, we're safe just going with number three.

> "Love your enemies, do good to those who hate you, bless those who curse you" (Luke 6:27–28). #Leadership endures personal wrongs.

## When Criticized, Just Do This

You may be the kind of person who has no problems wielding authority and being in command. But my guess is even you have doubts about your leadership.

It's normal to doubt at least occasionally. In reality, not everyone can be our raving fans. Some think we're weak, some mentally roll their eyes when we speak, others smile in the front and stab in the back. Even the most popular leaders have critics.

Can I tell you that you should self-doubt less often? As leaders we're going for the big picture. We should want *most* of our followers to like us, *most* of our strategies to work. We won't get a hit with every swing.

While people may not be happy with us all the time, they are not our first priority. We are first to be righteous—have right standing with God. This is the act of a servant leader: to obey our own King before we lead anyone else.

We wonder how to be servant leaders and yet be in control and in authority—this is how.

Let the critics criticize, but let the leader obey. It's ultimately for the people's good.

> When the godly are in authority, the people rejoice.
> (Prov. 29:2a, 1984 NIV)

## If You're Still Criticized . . .

Here are a few quick encouragements from Scripture. If one jumps out, put it on a sticky note or on your social media feed.

> "Do not repay evil with evil or insult with insult . . . but with blessing" (1 Pet. 3:9). Even when they criticize your #leadership!

> "If you suffer for doing good & endure it, this is commendable before God" (1 Pet. 2:20). A form of #leadership integrity.

> "For it is God's will that by doing good you should silence the ignorant talk of foolish people" (1 Pet. 2:15). Strike back with good!

> "If you are insulted because of the name of Christ, you are blessed" (1 Pet. 4:14). Have you been blessed lately?

The Apostle Paul shared our pain. He was the ultimate trail-blazer and rarely without detractors:

> "[A] great door for effective work has opened to me, and there are many who oppose me." (1 Cor. 16:9)

## Consistent Opposition Should Have One Result

In Numbers 16, several once-loyal followers of Moses rise up and incite hundreds of others to rebel with them.

> [3] They came as a group to oppose Moses and Aaron and said to them, "You have gone too far! The whole community is holy, every one of them, and the LORD is with them. Why then do you set yourselves above the LORD's assembly?"

This prideful mutiny reminds me of the "entitlement" mantra bandied about today. These people are blinded by it. But Moses attempts to bring them to their senses, exposing their selfish ambition and confronting them head on.

He doesn't turn the other cheek—he stands up against this insolence. It's a form of mercy because he knows if they go too far it could mean judgment from the Lord himself.

> [8] Moses also said to Korah, "Now listen, you Levites! [9] Isn't it enough for you that the God of Israel has separated you from the rest of the Israelite community and brought you near himself to do the work at the LORD's tabernacle and to stand before the community and minister to them? [10] He has brought you and all your fellow Levites near himself, but now you are trying to get the priesthood too. [11] It is against the LORD that you and all your followers have banded together. Who is Aaron that you should grumble against him?"
>
> [12] Then Moses summoned Dathan and Abiram, the sons of Eliab. But they said, "We will not come! [13] Isn't it enough that you have brought us up out of a land flowing with milk and honey to kill us in the wilderness? And now you also want to lord it over us!"

Moses sees that they won't back down, and he decides to begin their judgment himself.

> [15] Then Moses became very angry and said to the Lord, "Do not accept their offering. I have not taken so much as a donkey from them, nor have I wronged any of them."
> [16] Moses said to Korah, "You and all your followers are to appear before the Lord tomorrow—you and they and Aaron."

The next day, the Lord metes out his judgment, killing all those who opposed him and threatening the rest of the grumblers.

Is there anyone consistently opposing your leadership? If you sense insolence or resentment, first make sure you *deserve* to be followed. There may indeed be good reason people are resisting you.

If you find yourself being obedient to the Lord, it's time to release the disobedient from service. A leader should never tolerate open rebellion.

"Now Stephen, full of God's grace & power, did great wonders among the people. Opposition arose" (Acts 6:8). #Leadership draws opposition.

Facing opposition threatening you or your family? "The Lord will fight for you; you need only to be still" (Exod. 14:14).

## PART II

# Breaking Out:
# How to Develop
# Undeniable Boldness

## CHAPTER 5

# Necessary Division, Insult, and Conflict

## Introduction

> "In days to come you will understand this" (Jer. 30:24). #Leadership must at times do inexplicable things.

Jeremiah delivered a prophecy that contained such cryptic and unbelievable future events that the general populace could not possibly comprehend all its implications. It was as if he were a parent consoling his child with the equivalent of "This is for your own good. You'll understand why later."

Similarly, most leaders intellectually know people at the top must sometimes perform unsavory tasks for the good of those they lead and for the organization itself. But when they carry out such painful duties, they often grapple with the fact that no explanation will satisfy everyone.

Living and leading with such dissonance is necessary at times. This section explores several passages that help us prepare for the tension.

The first is a fact no one can escape, regardless of their religion:

> "In this world you will have trouble" (John 16:33).
> Wise #leadership realizes that trouble is no respecter of persons.

No matter who we are or what we believe, many of the biblical truths about leadership are undeniable.

> "And they lived in hostility toward all their brothers" (Gen. 25:18b). Some conflict will never be resolved.

> "Whoever says to the guilty, 'You are innocent,' will be cursed by peoples" (Prov. 24:24). #Leadership requires confronting wrongdoing.

## Sometimes the Leader Must Cause Division

Oh, how I hate to cause pain. When someone needs to be corrected, disciplined, or fired, my stress kicks in.

The Gospels indicate that though Jesus fought the Pharisees and resisted the Romans, he hated that part of his job. But he knew in order to bring about unity, he must first root out the chaff.

He called people fools, broods of vipers, faithless, hypocrites, and a "wicked generation." I am not saying he was cruel, insensitive, or compassionless. In each case, the so-named people were blaspheming God. Or they were deceiving the people. Or they were greedy, lustful, prideful.

Is there some kind of division needed in your organization? Who but the leader can effect it?

If a rift forms on its own apart from the leader, the more powerful people will win—not necessarily those who are in the right.

It's only the leader who can rightly divide.

> "Are you so foolish?" (Gal. 3:3). Sometimes #leadership requires such frankness.

## Don't Be Afraid to Insult People with the Truth

> "Have I now become your enemy by telling you the truth?" (Gal. 4:16). Hard truth must be spoken by #leadership.

Truth without love is brutality, and love without truth is hypocrisy.

—*Warren Wiersbe*

In Luke 11:37–54, Jesus shows a shocking side of himself. He accepts an invitation to dinner at a Pharisee's house, but instead of graciously accepting the hospitality and having a pleasant evening with his host, he insults the man.

An expert in the law reclining with them at the table says, "Teacher, when you say these things, you insult us also" (v. 45).

But rather than smoothing this unintended ruffled feather, Jesus fires another arrow: "And you experts in the law, woe to you, because you load people down with burdens they can hardly carry, and you yourselves will not lift one finger to help them."

When Jesus was done with these guys, he had made mortal enemies. Literally.

What did he gain from this risky confrontation?

What is to be gained from *any* confrontation? Think about your own life and work. What benefits have you seen from differences with people you're close to, or even with those who are mere acquaintances?

When there is reconciliation, the relationship benefits and even strengthens. Deeper intimacy results from the vulnerable baring of hearts and expression of inner truths.

Though the dinner host and his guests went to bed insulted, perhaps later on they meditated on Christ's words and reconciled with God.

Jesus modeled for us a law of leadership: We must deal in truth. When that truth insults someone, we can't shrink back.

The most courageous leaders in the world trust in truth and raise their voices in its defense.

> Instead, speaking the truth in love, we will grow to become in every respect the mature body of him who is the head, that is, Christ. (Eph. 4:15)

## Manage Shortcomings with Process

People, whether young or old, are made to disobey. It's a condition we all inherited from our father Adam. Human nature is naturally sinful and often forgetful of its sin.

Which is why we need all the help we can get with our sinful employees and volunteers. King Joash gives us an effective methodology in 2 Kings 12.

The king assigns his priests to repair the temple with funds collected from the people. But the priests mismanage the money and the king realizes he needs to scrap his strategy and start over.

So Joash puts a chest next to the altar for all to see, where the people put their offerings for the repair work. Now when the priests guarding the chest see it fill up, they alert the high priest, who brings the royal secretary to count it and bag it. They then dole out the money to the men supervising the work, who in turn pay the workers. They also purchase all the necessary materials and "met all the other expenses of restoring the temple" (v. 12).

The priests loved the temple. It was their pride in life, their purpose, and in fact their livelihood. You would assume they'd be the logical ones to fix the building—but they lacked the skills to manage tasks and money. Passion and purpose weren't enough; it took a new process to the get the job done.

When an area of your organization is chronically deficient, a process overhaul may be required.

Systems, rules, and procedures may not change human nature, but they at least improve the chances people will get the job done right.

## To Cast Vision, Be Prepared to Cause Division

"Do you think I came to bring peace on earth?
No, I tell you, but division."

—*Luke 12:51*

How could the Prince of Peace say this? The Son of God's purpose was to show the world God's love, wasn't it?

If you back up to verses 49 to 50, Jesus says, "I have come to bring fire on the earth, and how I wish it were already kindled! But I have a baptism to undergo, and what constraint I am under until it is completed!"

This sounds like a passionate leader intent on ushering in the wrath of God—not a gentle shepherd nurturing his flock. Yet we know this man by his compassion. He is characterized as turning the other cheek.

A few minutes later he would begin teaching the masses. The lessons would be hard; he planned to confront them in many ways.

Before he did this, he gathered his twelve disciples around him to prepare them for the difficult truths he was about to unveil. He would soon travel the countryside confronting, healing, and attracting the attention of the authorities, who would see him as a threat. His life would be in danger. There would be fire and division—not just love, healing, and salvation.

We see Jesus's raw emotion in verses 49 to 50 of The Message:

"I've come to start a fire on this earth—how I wish it were blazing right now! I've come to change everything, turn everything rightside up—how I long for it to be finished! Do you think I came to smooth things over and make everything nice? Not so. I've come to disrupt and confront!"

For the greater vision and the ultimate good of his people, Jesus was willing to light a blaze and confront all who opposed God. He knew, of course, that it would rip him and his disciples apart. But he looked ahead to the greater good.

Jesus's example gives me courage to not just cast a vision, but to risk for it and to cast passivity to the wind.

It also beckons me to look into the far future. One day God will review my leadership, my company, and how I lived my life.

Let's live and lead now as if our review meeting with God were just around the corner.

Because it is.

## Biblical Leaders Don't Have to Be Nice All the Time

I don't envy those of you in church leadership.

You have pressures those of us in the marketplace don't have. When you let a staff member go, you often have a tougher time because you've been at his family's hospital bedside, done their funerals, conducted their marriages, or counseled them through personal crises. When we part ways with employees, the roots aren't as deep, and the aftermath doesn't last as long or spread among entire families like in the church.

Whether you lead in ministry or any kind of organization, Solomon has some great advice (and I paraphrase): "Be nice. But sometimes don't be nice."

That's a relief on one hand—it's OK to not to be liked all the time. On the other, especially for us people pleasers, it's frightening. *What do you mean, don't be nice?* Most of us actually care about what people think.

Let's look at a passage in Ecclesiastes you've heard before:

### Ecclesiastes 3:1–8
[1] There is a time for everything,
    and a season for every activity under the heavens:
[2] a time to be born and a time to die,
    a time to plant and a time to uproot,
[3] a time to kill and a time to heal,
    a time to tear down and a time to build,
[4] a time to weep and a time to laugh,
    a time to mourn and a time to dance,
[5] a time to scatter stones and a time to gather them,
    a time to embrace and a time to refrain from embracing,
[6] a time to search and a time to give up,
    a time to keep and a time to throw away,
[7] a time to tear and a time to mend,
    a time to be silent and a time to speak,

[8] a time to love and a time to hate,
    a time for war and a time for peace.

Jesus himself said, "Do not suppose that I have come to bring peace to the earth. I did not come to bring peace, but a sword" (Matt. 10:34).

If you too must be a peacebreaker from time to time, remember you're in good company. Jesus showed the way we need to be when short-term peace is detrimental to the greater good.

## CHAPTER 6

# Toughness and Nerve

## Introduction

> "Be on your guard; stand firm in the faith; be men of courage; be strong" (1 Cor. 16:13).

On the topic of boldness, the Bible speaks to two types of people: those who aren't bold enough and those who are bold by nature.

It says that at times, both are in error. Even excessively bold believers—those we look up to as world changers—may need to recheck their motivations, just like the rest of us. There's the risk of pride on the action side of the coin, but on the other, fear can stifle us into inaction.

Chances are you're like me—somewhere in the middle. The unholy coupling of pride and fear dances in my head, one vying to lead the other depending on the song playing at the moment.

So how we do we consistently lay hold of the right kind of boldness? How do we check our ego and yet unleash our courage?

## Get Out of God's Way

Finding God's best for our leadership requires diligent attention to the spiritual side of boldness. We do well to start with recognizing the source of true toughness.

> "Some trust in chariots & horses, but we trust in the name of the Lord our God" (Ps. 20:7). #Leadership trusts God, not resources.

We have omnipotence on our side. But the Lord's strength is not characterized by quick reactions to attack or insult. On the contrary.

> "The Lord is slow to anger but great in power" (Nah. 1:3). God's #leadership quality should shape our own character.

This is God's way of boldness. Just as Jesus could have called down twelve legions of angels to defend him (Matt. 26:53)—but restrained himself in deference to God's greater plan—we are to check our anger before we act on it. What might God be doing that doesn't need our anger to accomplish?

Ultimately Jesus did more himself than a horde of angels could ever do. In one act, he completely defeated the enemy.

> "Having disarmed the powers & authorities . . .
> triumphing over them by the cross" (Col. 2:15). Jesus
> gives us power! #leadership

God's plan for his Son wasn't just victory over sin, but annihilation of all enemy forces. Now we as the Church are to execute our role as the conquering army occupying its new territory.

> "God did not give us a spirit of timidity, but of power,
> of love & of self-discipline" (2 Tim. 1:7). Top #leadership qualities.

At the end of the Bible, Jesus declares this absolute triumph yet again: "I am the Living One; I was dead, and now look, I am alive for ever and ever! And I hold the keys of death and Hades" (Rev. 1:18).

God's power is complete. Therefore, let us drop the illusion that we are strong in and of ourselves. He wants us to confidently rely on him.

> Remember who you are: "who thru faith are shielded by God's power" (1 Pet. 1:5). A comforting thought in #leadership.

## Be Strong and Still

> "Wait for the Lord; be strong & take heart & wait for the Lord" (Ps. 27:14). There's strength in waiting. #leadership

In this verse, David implores us to be strong while we wait on the Lord to act.

But even when we don't feel very strong, we can act and think as if we were.

When I got into radio advertising sales out of college, they trained us to smile into the phone; the person on the other end could "hear" us smiling, whether we actually felt happy or not. The silent smile erased verbal stress tones and projected an audible confidence.

When we act strong, it's as if we *are* strong. No one knows the difference. (Except us!)

Acting aside, there's an even greater imperative in the above verse. It's repeated twice for emphasis: "Wait for the Lord." It is in the waiting that we are strengthened, and it is this strength that enables us to keep waiting.

Later in Psalms, we encounter a complementary command:

> "Be still & know that I am God" (Ps. 46:10). Relax;
> we aren't in control. #leadership

We are told to simply be still (in other words, to wait.) And in our stillness, the verse exhorts us to calmly meditate on the fact that he is God.

As we wait for the Lord and meditate on him, he strengthens us, encourages us, and acts for us.

Do you need to wait—rather than act—on anything in your life right now?

## Be Strong and Go

Conversely, is it time to act? Have you been waiting, praying, and seeking counsel, and now you feel ready to move?

The Spirit often prompts action. When he declares the end of your waiting time, sometimes you feel it; a spiritual energy fuels you. Other times his whisper fills our sails and we naturally propel forward.

Of course, when we do nothing, God often acts on his own. It is his prerogative to do whatever, whenever. But after we place our confidence in the Lord and wait for him, he very well may send us out.

> "Be strong and do the work" (1 Chron. 28:10). King David's #leadership advice to his son; good for all of us.

When we obey his command to go, we must not only be strong, but look out for opposition:

> "And from the time John the Baptist began preaching until now, the Kingdom of Heaven has been forcefully advancing, and violent people are attacking it." (Matt. 11:12, NLT)

When Jesus came, he waged a campaign against Satan, who responded with cohorts of demons and men to reclaim his lost ground. The apostles operated on these front lines. Here was their reaction to enemy activity:

> "Lord, consider their threats & enable your servants to speak your word with great boldness" (Acts 4:29). #leadership

Their prayer moved God. "After they prayed," the Scripture says a few verses later, "the place where they were meeting was shaken. And they were all filled with the Holy Spirit and spoke the word of God boldly" (Acts 4:31).

As part of the Lord's advance army, we will be attacked. But as we march, the Sword of the Spirit should fill us with courage and boldness. Jesus said, "I will build my church, and all the powers of hell will not conquer it" (Matt. 16:18, NLT).

No power, no enemy can stand in the way of this force. Jesus *will* build his kingdom. Nothing will stand in its way.

What an inspiration for action.

Let's go!

## Be Boldly Unsure

> "Fight the good fight of faith" (1 Tim. 6:12). Faithful #leadership fights for—and with—faith.

Do any of us know what tomorrow brings? Of course not. We've got to take that action, make that hire, form that team, reassign that volunteer, cast that vision, all without 100 percent certainty how any of it will turn out.

A healthy leader must accept this personal inadequacy and expect people to fail us—even expect *ourselves* to fail at times. This drives us to become better leaders. It also drives us to our knees in prayer.

We should feel just uncomfortable enough with ourselves and our circumstances to seek continual improvement (and of course to rely on God more than ourselves).

Complacency is the enemy of growth. **Leaders must be boldly unsure.** Just about every major biblical leader exhibited this quality. Men like Noah, Moses, Joseph, Gideon, and David all charged ahead at different times in their lives even when they weren't sure of the outcome.

> "Now go; I will help you speak & will teach you what to say" (Exod. 4:12). When we are called to #leadership, he guides us.

## Lead in the Strength You Have

Some days I can scale the mountain of to-dos and appointments, but other days I'd rather walk down an easy path or just go home.

It's not an introversion versus extroversion thing; it's more of moods and energy. Sometimes I just feel weak. Think about your own rhythm: Are there certain days of the week or times of the day when you're more energetic? Do people's opinions or even the weather affect you?

Resilient leaders keep climbing when the cliff becomes sheer. We all like to think we're strong too.

But the fact is, sometimes we feel weak. I love the encouragement the Lord gives Gideon, a leader who readily admitted his weaknesses:

The LORD turned to him and said, "Go in the strength
you have and save Israel out of Midian's hand. Am I
not sending you?" (Judg. 6:14)

Whatever strength we possess is enough for Almighty God.
I wonder if Gideon's weaknesses—being from the smallest clan
in the smallest tribe—were exactly *why* God chose him to attack
the Midianites. If Gideon had been a great warrior from a long
line of conquering chieftains, everyone would've expected him
to be victorious. Not only did God choose a weak leader, he
forced Gideon to attack with a much smaller force than any sane
general would've taken into battle.

God will work out whatever victory he wants despite our
weaknesses. Therefore, we should accept our limitations—very
likely he has given them to us to force us to rely on him. We
should lead despite our weaknesses, with a divine, borrowed
strength.

I chuckle every time I read the verses just before this passage:

When the angel of the LORD appeared to Gideon, he
said, "The LORD is with you, mighty warrior."

"Pardon me, my lord," Gideon replied, "but if
the LORD is with us, why has all this happened to
us?" (Judg. 6:12–13)

An innocent question from someone used to being the underdog! I wonder the same thing sometimes.

Nevertheless, the Lord is with us, and his victory is sure.

> Allow yourself days when you're not Super Leader. The sun rises & falls; the tide goes in & out. #leadership

> When leaders feel inadequate, they're driven to become better. Occasional inadequacy is how #leadership stays sharp.

## CHAPTER 7

# Authority and Power

## Introduction

Alexander the Great conquered much of the known world 2,300 years ago and has commanded the world's respect ever since. He obsessed with besting his father Phillip's conquests and lived to carve his name into history, no matter how much carnage and mayhem he caused along the way.

If he hadn't possessed a royal lineage or strong army, would he still have become the Great? Perhaps he possessed such strong leadership qualities that he would've risen to prominence on his own. But the fact remains that his kingly authority derived from his father.

We who have been born again have a new Father ourselves, and we are righteous and royal regardless of our earthly heritage. We are called to live and lead in the power of our newly inherited Kingdom.

Have you grasped this divine authority?

> [I]n all these things we are more than conquerors
> through him who loved us (Rom. 8:37)

## Don't Suffer the Nonsense

Kathy is a great leader in our company. She commutes from Boston to our Louisville office about once a month. She always comments on the difference in culture between the Northeast and the South.

"Up there," she says, "we don't tolerate nonsense."

When she joined the company, she and I worked together to reduce the nonsense. I didn't realize how dysfunctional we had become.

You know what I mean by nonsense. Unnecessary or incessant drama. Infighting, jealousy, complaining, resistance, and all manner of irrational behavior.

The problem Kathy encountered was that despite the slower, softer pace and the kinder people, everyone danced around problems down here. No one dealt with things head on until they absolutely had to. Certain unacceptable behaviors were tolerated for too long.

When she came on board, this seasoned executive commanded the immediate respect of her staff. But rather than beat them into submission, she solved their toughest problems and called people out who needed some tough love.

The lesson for all of us in the South is simple: Deal with nonsense.

Kathy taught me to lower my threshold for foolish behavior. There's always room for grace, but when it comes to telling someone the truth and confronting an issue, Christian leaders hesitate to confront (even in the Northeast).

Many believers let stuff go because they think they're showing grace. But as biblical leaders, we have a responsibility to thoughtfully come out from behind this theological term and apply wisdom.

Folly can have serious consequences, especially if left unchecked.

Maybe that's why Proverbs 10:21 ends with "fools die for lack of sense."

## What Do You Worship? That's the Source of Your Leadership Power

When Jesus said in Matthew 28:18, "All authority in heaven and on earth has been given to me," he acknowledged that even he—the Son of God—had to receive his authority. He didn't assume it or take it.

Authority is tricky because most people think it means "authoritative." If someone is authoritative, he must be a leader and therefore must be obeyed.

But this kind of leadership doesn't last because true authority is spiritual. It's a matter of the spirit, not the job.

Spiritual authority is derived from worship. Who or what we worship has our permission to rule our hearts and give us power. Our deep-set desires spring from the object of our worship. And these desires always come out in our leadership, sometimes in destructive ways, sometime productive.

Let me illustrate with the five objects of worship.

**1. Worship of self**: Your power and authority come from your ego; you become a prideful leader. This is short-term leadership that never ends well.

> Do nothing out of selfish ambition or vain conceit. (Phil. 2:3)

> Pride goes before destruction, a haughty spirit before a fall. (Prov. 16:18)

**2. Worship of others**: Your authority comes from the permission of other people; you become a passive leader. Your lack of initiative may eventually disqualify you from leadership.

> Peter and the other apostles replied: "We must obey God rather than human beings!" (Acts 5:29)

**3. Worship of sin (and Satan)**: Your power comes from your lusts and desires, driving you to satisfy them; you become a slave to sin, a power-hungry and immoral leader.

The devil led [Jesus] up to a high place and showed him in an instant all the kingdoms of the world. And he said to him, "I will give you all their authority and splendor; it has been given to me, and I can give it to anyone I want to. If you worship me, it will all be yours." (Luke 4:5–7)

**4. Worship of money**: Your power grows the richer you get; you become a fearful leader, anxious about losing your treasure.

No one can serve two masters. Either you will hate the one and love the other, or you will be devoted to the one and despise the other. You cannot serve both God and money. (Matt. 6:24)

**5. Worship of the Lord**: Your power comes from God; you become a humble, authoritative leader.

For the LORD takes delight in his people; he crowns the humble with victory. (Ps. 149:4)

Followers grant the leader authority first because of position, then continue following if their interests are served.

Followers may not immediately see the source of the leader's own authority—thinking it's only because of position—but over time it becomes evident. When they realize the source (see the list above), our leadership is either diluted or cemented.

Think of a general who wins victories but who is later found out to be a self-serving megalomaniac who sacrificed the lives of his soldiers in order to claim victory for himself. What becomes of his leadership then?

When Jesus was tempted by Satan, our Lord made a statement that should define our own leadership and the source of our authority: "It is written: 'Worship the Lord your God and serve him only.' "

When our worship and service direct upward, the people around us follow our gaze.

## Follow This Equation to Powerful Leadership

A theme I hope you see throughout this book is that the most effective leaders serve with authority. Let me give you another example.

In 1 Chronicles 13:12, we read that "David was afraid of God that day." Why? Because the Lord judged disobedience with a flash of anger that resulted in the death of Uzzah, one of David's men.

After this, the Lord confirms that his seal of approval—and power—is upon King David:

> And David knew that the LORD had established him as king over Israel and that his kingdom had been highly exalted for the sake of his people Israel. (1 Chron. 14:2)

In the latter part of this verse we see that David's kingdom was highly exalted—in other words, given great power and authority—so that he might serve and protect his people.

After this, the king followed the Lord diligently, calling on him at crucial times. The result of this faithful leader grabbing hold of God and his authority is given several verses later:

> David's fame spread throughout every land, and the LORD made all the nations fear him. (1 Chron. 14:17)

God transferred some of his fearsomeness to his key man because that man inquired of him and obeyed him.

David's example gives us a simple equation: Fear God, lead as an authoritative servant, and God will fill you with *his* confidence, power, and strength.

## Do This with Your Power

> ". . . strengthened with all power according to his might so you may have great endurance & patience" (Col. 1:11). True #leadership power!

Colossians 1:11 says we can receive power directly from God's own strength. We also learned from King David the way to tap into it.

But as servant leaders, what do we *do* with this heavenly power? Isn't power the antithesis of servanthood?

The "so you may" in the verse above is the answer: Power should translate into endurance and patience.

Let's look at the practical working out of this spiritual power. Endurance and patience empower a leader

- when conflict arises,
- when a mediocre year drags on,
- when the team lags,
- when everyone is starting to lose hope and patience with each other,
- when tragedy strikes,
- when a competitor threatens,
- when the right new hire still hasn't shown up,
- when a star employee leaves,
- when the company feels weak, or
- when investors make demands.

Obviously, a weak leader would fail in these scenarios. During tough times, people want a strong leader who has endured worse situations and who can patiently look past panic to the other side.

What requires extra patience and endurance from you right now? Even if no great threat looms, perhaps this is a time to help your people deal with their own everyday difficulties by encouraging them to patiently endure.

> "God is working in you, giving you the desire & power to do what pleases him" (Phil. 2:13, NLT). #Leadership is letting God work through us.

> "We are God's workmanship, created in Christ Jesus to do good works, which God prepared in advance for us to do" (Eph. 2:10). #Leadership is discovering his plan.

## Four Ways Leaders Should Seek Personal Glory

We all know the servant leader eschews glory. For him or her, humility should come before honor (Prov. 18:12), never the reverse.

But there is a healthy glory the leader can seek. In fact, he *should* seek it.

Glory stems from the root idea of "heaviness" and indicates "weight" or "worthiness." It can describe a person's wealth, splendor, or reputation.

But rather than seeking to enrich our reputation or our coffers, God wants us to chase after spiritual glory in at least four ways:

1. **Nurture wisdom, patience, and peace.** Proverbs 19:11 says, "A person's wisdom yields patience; it is to one's glory to overlook an offense." Add to that Proverbs 20:3: "It is to one's honor to avoid strife, but every fool is quick to quarrel."

2. **Seek God's truths.** Proverbs 25:2 reads, "It is the glory of God to conceal a matter; to search out a matter is the glory of kings."

3. **Let God himself become your glory.** Psalm 3:3 reveals that God's strength fills us and surrounds us: "But you, LORD, are a shield around me, my glory, the One who lifts my head high."

4. **Accept the glory God has already bestowed upon you.** Psalm 8:5 (NLT) says, "Yet you made them only a little lower than God and crowned them with glory and honor."

As Psalm 103:4 says, Christian leaders are already crowned with love and compassion.

Let's lead with that glorious crown firmly in place.

## Establish and Practice Your Authority

People are inherently authority-based. The whole world runs on authority. You can't drive twenty feet without being under the authority of the speed limit, right of way, and other rules of the road. Government is nothing but an authoritative body that carries out certain functions.

As a leader, do you truly grasp the authority of your position? It has been given to you with certain requirements and responsibilities. If you're a senior pastor, committee leader, or a consultant, you have a prescribed level of authority. People expect certain things from you, and they have a threshold of tolerance for anything you might do within the bounds of your position.

Have you fully inhabited the positions of authority you occupy in all areas of your life? Are there any areas where you're too passive?

Let's look at some verses from the New Living Translation that help us understand God's view of authority.

> **1 Chronicles 26:6**: Shemaiah had sons with great ability who earned positions of great **authority** in the clan.

> **Esther 8:11**: The king's decree gave the Jews in every city **authority** to unite to defend their lives.

> **Proverbs 29:2**: When the godly are in **authority**, the people rejoice. But when the wicked are in power, they groan.

> **Matthew 10:1**: Jesus called his twelve disciples together and gave them **authority** to cast out evil spirits and to heal every kind of disease.

**Matthew 16:1**: One day the Pharisees and Sadducees came to test Jesus, demanding that he show them a miraculous sign from heaven to prove his **authority**.

**Matthew 28:18**: Jesus came and told his disciples, "I have been given all **authority** in heaven and on earth."

**Luke 7:8**: I know this because I am under the **authority** of my superior officers, and I have **authority** over my soldiers.

**Romans 13:1**: Everyone must submit to governing **authorities**. For all **authority** comes from God, and those in positions of **authority** have been placed there by God.

**1 Peter 2:13**: For the Lord's sake, submit to all human **authority**.

There are three things to notice in these passages:

1. Everyone is under some other authority. Everyone.
2. Authority is given to people; you can't create it for yourself.
3. People earn the authority given to them.

These verses give us a picture of servant leadership but also of serving with *authority*. When we are given a position that carries a certain scope of authority, we are meant to exercise it. To be passive is to be disobedient and shirk our duty; we must enter into the power given us and perform as the higher authority over us expects.

As servant leaders, we serve not only the people who follow us, but we serve those over us—and ultimately, we serve God. Servanthood looks different in all three of these cases:

1. **Serving followers**: Protect them, meet their needs, guide them, give them clarity of purpose, encourage them, discipline them, give them meaningful work.
2. **Serving those over us**: Be obedient; go the extra mile to do more than asked.
3. **Serving God**: Heed his will more so than our own or anyone else's; listen for his voice, obey even when it doesn't make sense; have faith; worship him; become a true servant to his people; sacrifice our desires and die to ourselves.

There are, of course, many similarities between serving the authorities over us and serving God as our ultimate authority.

Authority starts with him and cascades down through generations and organizations and families and churches. He is the spring that turns into a river that becomes a waterfall.

How should we wield our authority when it comes to managing our staff? Is there a single biblical prescription that we can tack up on our wall and remind ourselves of every morning?

I'm going to offer you one:

**I build my authority by building other people up.**

This is a biblical philosophy of authority for dealing with staffing issues. It's based on two verses:

> I may seem to be boasting too much about the authority given to us by the Lord. But our authority builds you up; it doesn't tear you down. So I will not be ashamed of using my authority. (2 Cor. 10:8, NLT)

> I am writing this to you before I come, hoping that I won't need to deal severely with you when I do come. For I want to use the authority the Lord has given me to strengthen you, not to tear you down. (2 Cor. 13:10, NLT)

When we build people up, our authority grows in the eyes of those we lead. Then, when we need to do something difficult, we have the trusted authority to do so.

## I build my authority by building other people up <u>now</u>.

I want to stress that additional word on the end—"now." We build now for later use. We invest now for a future return. We sow now so we can reap later. We work now in anticipation of receiving our wages later. We must build people up *now*.

The opposite is true too: We *lose* authority when all we do is tear people down. There are consequences for current actions. It's like building up debt that we keep putting off until the bill becomes so big it drives us to bankruptcy. It's like living your own life without any belief in God, and when you get to the other side, you're surprised by his judgment.

How many times have you either been under a leader or observed a leader that habitually tore people down, and ultimately those people left?

How will you build up the people who follow you? Think of some new ways to encourage them. You can give them an important assignment and trust them to do it. You can go on vacation and put things in their hands for a few days. You can promote them. You can simply greet them and make them feel like you care. There are lots of ways to build someone up.

Wield your authority to build your people, and they'll in turn build the organization. This is what leadership is all about.

When you empower others, your own power increases. #leadership

Instruction does much, but encouragement everything.

—*Johann Wolfgang von Goethe*

## CHAPTER 8

# Gentle Strength

## Introduction

> Patient persistence pierces through indifference;
> gentle speech breaks down rigid defenses.
> —*Proverbs 25:15 (The Message)*

In the NIV, the first half of Proverbs 25:15 explains that even the most indifferent and hard-to-please people—such as those in royalty—can fall prey to patient persistence: "Through patience a ruler can be persuaded."

Many leaders striving to serve discover there is strength in patience and gentleness. The art of servant leadership, however, hinges on when and how such restraint is applied.

## Establish a Balance of Power

If you took an inventory of your personal leadership style, you'd probably find yourself leaning toward gentleness or forcefulness rather than right down the middle. I tend toward being too gentle in situations that require stronger engagement. I know other leaders that hit everything with a hammer. Jesus was a master at knowing what kind of persuasive power to employ in any given circumstance.

So we're left with the quest for balance. The Bible explores this by encouraging us to lay a foundation of gentleness.

> "Everyone should be quick to listen, slow to speak and slow to become angry" (Jas. 1:19).

> "Let your gentleness be evident to all" (Phil. 4:5). Even as a leader!

> How to lead right now: "Be completely humble and gentle; be patient, bearing with one another in love" (Eph. 4:2).

Gentleness is easy to spot, simple to understand.

Though not so easy to practice.

## Use the (Gentle) Force

> Then Jesus entered the Temple and began
> to drive out the people selling animals for
> sacrifices.
>
> —*Luke 19:45 (NLT)*

Whether you're a Star Wars fan or not, you've heard someone say, "Use the force." Luke the apostle (not the Jedi) saw Jesus use force to great effect as he sought to bring peace to the Temple of the Lord. The moment required a violent disruption of the merchants taking advantage of God's people.

We can use similar force to bring about God's peace:

> A gentle answer turns away wrath, but a harsh word
> stirs up anger. (Prov. 15:1)

Such force, of course, begins with a foundation of gentleness. When there's too much leaderly shouting going on day after day, followers' ears chafe and deafen. They tend to look for a softer voice of reason.

> The quiet words of the wise are more to be heeded
> than the shouts of a ruler of fools. (Eccl. 9:17)

In leadership, gentleness is complicated. When we are known as gentle, an occasional flare of anger in our voice perks people to attention. But the Bible doesn't teach that we should strategically get angry in order to accomplish our goals.

We lead with gentleness whenever possible, always in love. Sometimes with a passion that enforces our will.

## The Gentle Warrior

We'll never perfect the balance. But we can work hard to build gentleness into our personality, style, and practice.

With Jesus living inside us, we feel his peace inside our very souls: "Take my yoke upon you and learn from me, for I am gentle and humble in heart, and you will find rest for your souls" (Matt. 11:29).

Paul and Peter modeled how to lead with a strong personality. They left us numerous bits of advice on living as passionate, gentle, strong leaders:

> **Colossians 3:12:** Therefore, as God's chosen people, holy and dearly loved, clothe yourselves with compassion, kindness, humility, gentleness and patience.

> **1 Timothy 6:11:** But you, man of God, flee from all this, and pursue righteousness, godliness, faith, love, endurance and gentleness.

**1 Peter 3:14–15:** But in your hearts revere Christ as Lord. Always be prepared to give an answer to everyone who asks you to give the reason for the hope that you have. But do this with gentleness and respect . . .

One final question many strong leaders ask is how gentle speech helps in chaotic environments such as the battlefield or sports arena or in any high-octane office environment.

Solomon offers a succinct answer:

> "A gentle tongue can break a bone" (Prov. 25:15).
> Gentleness strengthens #leadership.

**Part III**

# Practicing Excellence: How to Apply Biblical Wisdom to Leadership Performance

# CHAPTER 9

# Mission, Vision, and Culture

## Introduction

> "All the believers were one in heart and mind" (Acts 4:32). #Unity results from bold #leadership.

The ultimate culture in any organization emphasizes unity. In fact, the specific vision almost doesn't matter if a group is unified in whatever they're doing.

Negativity and selfishness have a negative power over vision and unity. James gives us a picture:

> "Where you have envy & selfish ambition, there you find disorder . . ." (Jas. 3:16). Stamp out egos to bring order.

Negativity and ego trump unity, leading to chaos. In this verse, "disorder" is the antithesis of healthy leadership. When I don't lead well, my followers go in every which direction.

However you define vision, culture, and mission, one thing is clear: Unity is a necessary ingredient.

## Culture Isn't a Thing, It's a Result

Think about what makes up the culture in any organization—things like

- the character and personality of the leader,
- the physical environment,
- the types of hires usually made,
- whether the "mockers" have been expelled,
- how empowered and confident people are allowed to be,
- the communication style of the top leaders,
- how things get done,
- the industry you're in,
- how your business is doing,
- whether you're merging with another organization,
- geographic location,
- size of the organization, or
- the age of the organization.

These are just a few factors that contribute to culture. You could list another dozen, I'm sure.

If you want to change culture, just remember—it's extremely difficult. It is the logical result of numerous factors working together, many of which are out of your control. Who's in what position could be the most controllable—and impactful—change you can effect.

Culture isn't a thing, it's a result.

> Why do they say #culture trumps #vision? Why do #mission & vision have to be separate? The longer I lead, the more I wonder.

## Two Tactics That Shift Culture

We hear how difficult changing culture or introducing a new vision is in an organization. But I believe in most cases, change flows naturally out of a couple key leadership pivots.

**Pivot #1: People Placement**—We underwent management personnel changes a few years ago that drastically altered the feel of our company. I did very little to address culture after the new people came on board. They changed the environment without even knowing it, and I felt freer to recast a vision many had forgotten.

**Pivot #2: Happy Hearts**—If you feel like you've done all the people development and change-outs you can, Proverbs offers a simple tactic to soothe the culture:

> Want a shift in culture? Don't use words! "A cheerful look brings joy to the heart" (Prov. 15:30). #leadership

Sometimes we're too serious as we lead. Little things like smiles or greetings can affect people's moods. When I shoehorn myself out of my office and walk around, I find my own spirits lifting as people give *me* cheerful looks.

Even in a large company, where unique subcultures develop in departments, geographies, or divisions, a leader can affect her department's environment regardless of the overall corporate culture.

When the atmosphere seems stagnant or in decline, investing in motivational programs or workplace amenities could be a waste of time. Culture won't really change unless the people change first.

## Do You *Really* Lead with Clarity?

Clarity is rarely a conscious goal for leaders, yet every leader is consciously aware of its absence.

Clarity is a state of mind first achieved by the leader, then the followers, then customers.

Why is it so important? Consider all the areas of leadership where it's necessary—and where its nonexistence leaves a vacuum.

- Clarity in relationships
- Clarity in job descriptions and assignments
- Clarity in vision
- Clarity in delegation
- Clarity in communication
- Clarity in conflict
- Clarity in celebration
- Clarity in strategy
- Clarity of authority

If ambiguity rules in these areas, people will feel like they're not being led well. They naturally seek clarity, even if unconsciously so. They like to know what they're supposed to be doing, where they should be going.

Not that they want to be micromanaged, of course. The clarity they desire is an understanding of expectations and purpose.

Clarity is better than simplicity. Simple is good but not necessary. If an employee understands a new concept, it may still seem complex to outsiders, but now she can help them understand it too.

Clarity is not necessarily obvious. It stands on its own. It is fact. It is truth. It is memorable. It is easily memorized.

It is a journey from complexity, chaos, falsehoods, confusion, and conflict to comprehension. To "Aha!"

It is a process of removing obstacles that demotivate, demoralize, and derail.

Clarity sells.

Clarity motivates.

Clarity is clear vision.

Clarity cuts through the clutter.

Clarity clears the air.

Clarity removes the cloud so you can see the mountaintop.

> Clarity is coming, but not now. "Now I know in part; then I shall know fully . . ." (1 Cor. 13:12).

## Build a Cast of Stars before You Cast a Starry Vision

Is searching for a new "vision" the answer to most of the problems in your organization? The search for a compelling vision too often diverts energy from developing quality staff. Many times, "bad vision" is an excuse for a staff's shortcomings.

Excellence requires good execution by good people. If people aren't in the right positions, or processes are causing bottlenecks, or some people need to leave, a new vision is not necessarily the answer. It may seem like it is at first, but it will probably be sabotaged by the same things that are derailing the current vision.

First fix current problems—people, processes, structure, or resources. Fixing problems energizes people. When they're energized, they feel more motivated.

A motivated staff can more easily help the leader discover a new vision at the right time. **Build a cast of stars before you cast a starry vision.**

## Raise Your Vision

The Bible has much to say about vision. The problem, of course, with casting vision is that only God knows the future, and whether we prefer a certain future over another really doesn't matter in the end.

So what do we do with vision? We can't ignore it. It's hard to control. We surely can't see the future.

If we redefine vision as a goal that will glorify God, we get closer to God's own vision for our leadership.

The following shareable thoughts explore several ways to look at #vision.

> What if my grand #vision were to simply execute the current plan as successfully as possible? #leadership

> What motivates me in my work? The opportunity to create a future guided by God. #leadership

> Excitement about the future (which some call #vision) fuels my daily #leadership. What stokes you?

Down because you don't have a compelling #vision? Success & fulfilling work can inspire people until a vision emerges.

"Set your minds on things above, not on earthly things" (Col. 3:2). When #leadership looks up & beyond, others' eyes will follow.

"Let this be written for a future generation, that a people not yet created may praise the Lord" (Ps. 102:18). #vision #leadership

## CHAPTER 10

# Staffing

## Introduction

> "Then Moses cried out to the Lord, 'What am I to do with these people?'" (Exod. 17:4) The cry of those in #leadership!

*What am I to do with these people?* Indeed! I ask myself this question about once a month. People confound me. They surprise and disappoint me. They sometimes sadden me.

But they also step up and take charge. They're loyal and kind. They make my job easier. They make me laugh.

How do we know how to deal with people when they're such a mixed bag? How can any one leadership style effectively corral such diversity?

The first leadership task is to recognize that I'm mixed up too. Everyone says, "No one's perfect," but we're so far from perfect that this quaint little idiom gives us too much credit. My moods, fatigue, worries, workload, and any number of factors waylay me just when I need to be on my game.

Sometimes I'm glad I'm the leader because I know I'd be hard to manage. I ask the Holy Spirit all the time to fill me with compassion, energy, love, and joy. What spiritual needs do you have?

Our people are no different.

> "From now on we regard no one from a worldly point of view" (2 Cor. 5:16). People's faults hide their spiritual needs.

## Subordinate Words to Deeds

Mothers around the world have been right all along: People's actions speak louder than their words.

> [L]et us not love with words or speech but with actions and in truth. (1 John 3:18)

What we do proves who we are more than our words ever could. In the verse above, actions prove and purify our love. This verse from James says actions also prove our faith.

> What good is it, my brothers and sisters, if someone claims to have faith but has no deeds? (Jas. 2:14)

When employees say nice things and promise good intentions, it's action we must look for. I've been duped countless times by someone's well-meaning words, only to be followed by no action (or the wrong action). To me it's a matter of integrity—do what you say you're going to do.

What about your own words and deeds? Do they match up? Does one prove the other?

## Adopt New Action

When we start focusing on our actions and not just our words, we naturally wonder what we should be doing that we weren't doing before. The following shortlist includes a few biblical leadership best practices.

### 1. Be generous to a fault.

One of the most meaningful (and underrated) leadership activities is generosity. People tend to crave it from their leader when it's absent but take it for granted when it's routine. Let's let Scripture guide the balance in our own leadership.

"Do not withhold good from those who deserve it" (Prov. 3:27). A #leadership law that never fails.

"Do not hold back the wages of a hired man over-night" (Lev. 19:13). Pay people ASAP!

"As we have opportunity, let us do good to all people . . ." (Gal. 6:10) Especially employees who ask for help. #leadership

"Blessed are those who have regard for the weak; the Lord delivers them in times of trouble" (Ps. 41:1).

Worried about an earthly return? "Good will come to those who are generous and lend freely" (Ps. 112:5).

## 2. Don't be taken.

Many leaders are gullible at least some of the time. I have to remind myself when I'm listening to someone's complaints that there's another side to the story.

> "The first to present his case seems right, till another comes forward & questions him" (Prov. 18:17). #Leadership hears both sides.

### 3. Don't always strive to be liked.

In Nehemiah 13, Governor Nehemiah is finished with the wall around Jerusalem and has resumed his post at King Artaxerxes's side in Babylon. But from a distance he sees some of the Israelites back home going soft on God's law and neglecting the temple. So he asks the king if he can return to set his people straight.

He goes back to his hometown and does some tough stuff. He forces a leader out of the temple, commands people to get back to their posts, rebukes the nobles for desecrating the Sabbath, threatens to arrest merchants waiting like vultures outside the city gates on the Sabbath, and beats and calls down curses on men who married foreign women.

Nehemiah did what needed to be done. But by the end of the chapter, you get the picture he didn't feel particularly liked after enacting all this reform. He appeals to the Lord to validate his zeal:

> "Remember me with favor, my God" (Neh. 13:31). Nehemiah's prayer after tough #leadership people issues.

May we, too, do what's necessary, at the risk of not being liked. And may we look upward for approval.

## 4. Let people work for their reward.

I get a tic when people demand promotions. By the very act of asking for higher positions, they disqualify themselves as servant leaders.

When they ask for additional *responsibilities*, that's a different story. It's like one of King David's eager leaders who volunteered to lead the charge on Jebus, a city that would be renamed Jerusalem. This leader, Joab, risked his life for his king and was rewarded.

> "Whoever leads the attack . . . will become commander-in-chief" (1 Chron. 11:6). People should EARN #leadership roles.

While Joab knew what the reward would be, he responded to the need rather than asking for the role. David made him commander of the royal army.

## 5. Identify changed people by their overflow.

People typically won't change unless something dramatic (like God's hand) transforms them. But people do change: The Lord shook Saul, a sworn enemy of God's people, overnight.

> "You've heard of my previous way of life . . . how intensely I persecuted the church of God & tried to destroy it" (Gal. 1:13). #Leadership admits faults.

I've seen someone recover from an addictive lifestyle only to fall back into it over the ensuing years. He experienced severe misfortune and depression, pushing him right up to the edge. Fortunately, the Lord turned him around, and his faith is now stronger than it's ever been.

When someone changes for the good, be on the lookout for the overflow. Who they are will leak into their words and deeds in ways they can't control.

This is what happens to all of us who are saved and filled with the Holy Spirit.

> As for you, you were dead in your transgressions and sins, in which you used to live when you followed the ways of this world . . . (Eph. 2:1–2a)

## View Your Organization as a Blob

Organizations are like amoebas, constantly changing, splitting, moving, reshaping, on the brink of multiplying or dying.

It's useful to consider them this way rather than merely as a multilayered hierarchy. Think of a web of relationships instead of an organized list of titles and responsibilities.

We change our small company's structure sometimes based on the talent we find. One recent hire came in to replace an outgoing executive. The new guy instantly forged relationships and brought fresh energy to the role. His talents were different than the last guy's, too, which prompted us to change his job description. We even started a new line of business based on his abilities and work ethic.

If all you have are slots that need to be filled, you might be missing an opportunity to grow and change if you don't allow your people's personalities and skills to influence the business.

Of course, this kind of thinking is akin to seeing your company like the weather: unpredictable, seasonal, extreme, full of energy, prone to sudden beauty or darkness.

That's business.

And life.

## Do You Have an A Team?

I'd like to ask you a few questions:

1. Do you look at your current staff as an A team?
2. If not, what are you doing about it?
3. Is there a weak area of your leadership that may be causing problems among your team?

Several years ago, there was an executive at our company (let's call him John) who had simply been with us too long. I inherited him as part of the management team after I became CEO. His former boss had left the company. Many people, including John himself, assumed I would let him go after I settled into my new role.

Even though I wanted to, I couldn't make the change right away. One of my other senior leaders had made personnel changes of his own, and he thought if I made this move now, the company would have too much turnover at one time.

John at one point literally said to someone, "I don't know why I run all these reports and do these projects. No one ever looks at them or cares what I do." Wow—that said a lot. He himself didn't see his position fitting in the company.

I had made the mistake of letting him come in day after day, assuming he was being useful without much direction from me. Shame on me for letting it go on so long. I should've held him more accountable or ended things sooner.

If there are staffing issues in an organization, there are likely leadership issues at the top. If there are leadership issues at the top, there are likely also staffing issues.

"Your own conduct & actions have brought this upon you" (Jer. 4:18). #Leadership allows consequences.

"When wickedness comes, so does contempt . . . (Prov. 18:3). Be careful who you allow on your team.

## CHAPTER 11

# Success

## Introduction

Throughout history, the world has produced iconic leaders in every sector: military, literary, political, polemic, academic, scientific, musical, medical, technical, cinematic, athletic, artistic, entrepreneurial, financial, religious, royal, and industrial. You could probably pick a famous name in each.

Myriad authors and consultants have sought to dissect the elements of success from such leaders. What made Lincoln, MacArthur, Mozart, Einstein, and Curie tick? People at the pinnacle of success have much to teach, regardless of their field.

The Bible speaks to success as well. Let's listen to some advice from the divine Author of success.

## Delight in the Lord

> "Delight yourself in the Lord and he will give you the desires of your heart" (Ps. 37:4). Even my #leadership goals & desires.

What is your most inspiring vision right now? What are the goals you most want to achieve? Is there a dream driving you out of bed each morning?

What makes a leader is his or her daily striving. But as we yearn to succeed, God wants something beyond progress. He wants us to delight in him.

Does that sound sort of soft? "Delightful" is not a word that energizes me. But when we focus that delight on God by trusting, obeying, and loving him, he has an amazing promise: **He will give us the desires of our heart.**

As we persevere toward progress, let's delight in the Lord. Let's find pleasure in him, even as he finds pleasure in us:

> May these words of my mouth and the meditations
> of my heart be pleasing in your sight. (Ps. 19:14)

As our relationship deepens in this way, he'll grant us our deepest desires.

## Follow Divine Detours

> "All those who were in distress or in debt or discontented gathered around him, and he became their commander" (1 Sam. 22:2). David's #leadership restart.

David was a wanted man with a price on his head. While most upstanding citizens fled his path, many desperate people saw him as their hope. They knew he was trustworthy, but they also related to him because he had no refuge.

David's life had morphed from a nobody to national hero to innocent fugitive. He must've wished he'd never volunteered to fight that giant. Yet God had plucked him from obscurity and placed him in the limelight.

Why would the Lord allow his anointed to run scared just before placing him on the throne?

There was a greater plan at work. David's patience, trust, and faithfulness were tested and ultimately rewarded.

Sometimes, on the way to success, God drops a detour sign in our path.

## Excuse Your Weaknesses

> #Leadership weaknesses in one situation can be assets in another, like a victorious general who flounders during peacetime.

Where are you weakest in your leadership? Do you lack skill in planning, speaking, writing, socializing, numbers, people issues, or task focus?

Well, big deal. So you're not good at something. Neither were countless war heroes (including Winston Churchill) during peacetime. The sense of urgency and impending disaster that drew people to them in wartime dissipated afterward, when new leaders—the rebuilders—took precedence.

"Hero leaders" rise up at specific times for specific purposes. Then there's the rest of us. We lead in good times and bad, peacetime and war, day in and day out.

If I were called to leadership because history required my skills and personality for a specific mission, I'd feel much more useful than I do on any given day of my normal life.

So let's let ourselves have weaknesses.

Our strengths will lead us to success in due time, Lord willing.

> "If anyone is never at fault in what he says, he is a perfect man" (Jas. 3:2b). Relax—imperfection is OK!

## Recycle What Works

What has been will be again, what has been done will be done again . . .

—*Ecclesiastes 1:9*

Short on new ideas? Look to the past.

The market has been innovating and thinking outside the box for decades. But when we dissect our businesses and explore their history, we often discover core products, services, or models that have always delivered.

The technology, style, and context may change, but the basic ideas that drove past successes usually will still work.

I'm not talking about startups but rather businesses in stable industries looking for the next new thing. If that describes your organization, what core strategies and tactics have always delivered and simply need to be updated?

Sometimes the past truly is prelude to today's success.

## Value Experience Over Enthusiasm

> "The end of a matter is better than its beginning . . ."
> (Eccles. 7:8). #Leadership keeps the endgame in
> mind.

Do you agree with these statements about life and work?

- Age is more valuable than youth.
- Wisdom is more valuable than knowledge.
- Experience is more valuable than training.
- Achievement is more desirable than striving.

It's hard to argue that age, experience, and wisdom don't win in the end. As I've gotten older myself, I've learned the wisdom of hiring older people who may not have the energy they once had but who can leverage the past.

For the Christ-follower, leaving this earth is better than entering it.

The end of a matter is better than its beginning indeed.

## Prevent Partnership Failures

Leaders, "do not be yoked together with unbelievers" (2 Cor. 6:14). Badly yoked partnerships don't end well.

I can tell you from experience, this kind of failure hurts. Avoid it by waiting until you know your beliefs and even your goals line up with the other person's.

## Give

"Don't forget to do good & share with others, for with such sacrifices God is pleased" (Heb. 13:16). A calling of #leadership.

God's approval is a mark of success. We may generate lots of profit, grow an international brand, or plant a network of churches, but in the end, how does God see such accomplishments?

He sees them as good things, but according to the Hebrews verse above, that's only half the equation; we are also to sacrificially share what we have.

Giving is an undeniable responsibility of leadership. The world agrees with this, even expects it.

God exhibits this kind of giving. He has given us a position, resources, and a mission. He's given us mercy, grace, and the Holy Spirit, and has sacrificed his very Son for us.

When we sacrifice for others, we are recalling Jesus's ultimate gift of his life for us. Let's not serve our employees just because servanthood is the latest leadership fad; let's serve them because it pleases the Father.

> If you lend money to one of my people among you who is needy, do not treat it like a business deal; charge no interest. (Exod. 22:25)

## Beware Borrowing

> The borrower is slave to the lender.
> —*Proverbs 22:7b*

Years ago I asked some successful Christian executives their opinion on the scriptural validity of borrowing money to grow a business. I was torn between Dave Ramsey's no-debt approach to personal finance, and on the other hand the opportunity cost of never leveraging corporate growth. Here are a few notable answers to my question.

1. I think Romans 13:8 would say no ("Let no debt remain outstanding"). Whether that is reality in today's business world, I do not know. My only advice would be for you to consider carefully counting the cost . . . and then lay it all out before God and ask him for an answer.

2. I would think that it is OK to borrow for growth. The difference is between borrowing for consumption versus borrowing for investment. There is, of course, still risk, and so prudence is required, but I don't think borrowing for acquisition would be inherently sinful.

3. My understanding of the biblical position is that borrowing is permitted but should be done cautiously and prudently. The two definite prohibitions of borrowing are (1) if it enslaves the borrower, and (2) if usurious interest is paid.

The Bible doesn't teach that debt is wrong, just that it's dangerous and something to be forgiven when conscience requires. (God forgave our debts, didn't he?) Interesting that the longest debts in ancient Israelite communities lasted only seven years before they were forgiven (see Deut. 15:1).

So the counsel of these leaders and of Scripture is that we should avoid debt if we can, and when we do decide to employ other people's money, we should seek fast freedom before the chains of debt tighten.

Let no debt remain outstanding, except the continuing debt to love one another, for whoever loves others has fulfilled the law (Rom. 13:8).

## Rightly Measure Success

Sir Laurence Olivier was asked what made him such a successful actor. He said, "Humility enough to prepare and confidence enough to pull it off."

We have a responsibility as God's people not to think too highly of ourselves. Of course, belittling ourselves isn't right, either. The balance is to think of ourselves objectively, or as Romans 12:3 says, "think of yourself with sober judgment."

What does it mean as a servant leader to think of oneself with sober judgment? Let's look at two other translations of this verse:

Be honest in your evaluation of yourselves, measuring yourselves by the faith God has given us. (NLT)

In The Message, we read:

The only accurate way to understand ourselves is by what God is and by what he does for us, not by what we are and what we do for him.

The point is, no matter how much (or little) we do, we shouldn't measure our personal success by it. In fact, the word *success* in its traditional sense belittles God.

Instead, he wants us to watch what *he* does and give him glory for it. We are like his hands and feet, nothing more.

If we relax in his will and drink in the faith he pours in, we'll participate in his glory.

> "Be honest in your evaluation of yourselves . . ."
> (Rom. 12:3, NLT). Let's not kid ourselves about
> ourselves! #leadership

## Part IV

# Going Deep: How to Develop Spiritual Leadership in Yourself and Others

## CHAPTER 12

# Calling and Legacy

## Introduction

Our calling is not always clear. Consider one of God's beloved leaders:

> "After 40 years had passed, an angel appeared to Moses in the flames of a burning bush" (Acts 7:30). His #leadership moment finally came!

What do you think was on Moses's mind those forty years? I bet he doubted God at times. Maybe he was even bitter. But his day finally came in a most dramatic way.

Even after Moses had his burning-bush experience and accepted his assignment, the leadership challenges never ceased.

"Moses thought his own people would realize God was using him to rescue them, but they didn't" (Acts 7:25). Like Jesus!

Jesus led despite being misunderstood and without knowing exactly what the future held. "But about that day or hour no one knows, not even the angels in heaven, nor the Son, but only the Father" (Matt. 24:36).

When I hear people talk about receiving a life calling, I have a mixed response. On one hand, I understand what it feels like to be doing what God intended for you to do, what he *designed* you to do. But I also have to wonder if the person is simply justifying their current direction—maybe even rationalizing that what they want to do *must* be their calling.

Either way, there is a daily calling that holds true for all believers:

"Always give yourselves fully to the Lord's work, because you know your labor in the Lord is not in vain" (1 Cor. 15:58).

Regardless of the changing "callings" on our lives, if we put our hearts into them, our work is not in vain.

> "Remember me with favor, O God, for all I have done for these people" (Neh. 5:19). The prayer of servant #leadership.

In practical terms, calling is subjective, changing, sometimes thankless, always involving faith. It's that unknown aspect that requires our trust and reliance.

> "Who knows but that you have come to your royal position for such a time as this?" (Est. 4:14). Why might you REALLY be in #leadership?

It's impossible to know God's purposes in every situation we'll encounter in leadership. Sometimes he chooses not to reveal his plan in its entirety until more of it unfolds. So what to do?

> So whether you eat or drink or whatever you do, do it all for the glory of God. (1 Cor. 10:31)

Whatever we do, we must glorify him as we do it.

And yet many of us are still left yearning for specific direction. I hate making mistakes, wasting time and resources, and not moving forward on the right path. I bet you do too. I want to glorify the Lord, but I want to do it right.

## Heed the Law of Effective Work

"Lord, what do you want me to do?"

The question rings through the mind of every Christian leader on a regular basis. How to handle the problem employee? What overall strategy to employ? When to launch the new product? Who to hire? How much to spend?

Why do direction and guidance seem so elusive at times?

While I don't have space here to flesh out the entire biblical prescription for seeking the Lord in every issue, there *is* a simple way to know what we're supposed to be doing in a general sense.

The big questions of calling, ministry, vocation, mission, planning, and the like fall under the purview of what I call the Law of Effective Work.

When faced with a question of where to go or what to do next, we should look at all the doors in front of us. Some are barred, closed, cracked, ajar, or wide open. Which one should you walk through?

The one where you can do the most effective work.

The Apostle Paul originated this concept:

"[A] great door for effective work has opened to me . . ." (1 Cor. 16:9)

He went where he was led, where he was needed, where he was invited. Once he surrendered to the Lord, God used his skills in exciting new ways. He took Paul on life-threatening adventures. He gave him power and wisdom, and launched his leadership on an international scale.

Who is approaching you for help? What new business idea won't let you sleep at night? How has God gifted you? What opportunity has fallen into your lap? What exciting challenge is beckoning?

Ultimately where do you sense the Holy Spirit leading you? Is there an obvious way to glorify God right in front of you?

Look for the open doors. Look for opportunities to do effective work. Roll up your sleeves.

Then step through in faith.

## Leave Results to Someone Else

Several years ago, I listened to a brilliant leadership podcast by Andy Stanley. He said, "Be obedient to God and trust him with the consequences. Live your life as if truly God will take full responsibility for your leadership results."

Does this mean we should just relax and go with the flow? No. We have to disrupt. We have to innovate. We have to confront. We have to encourage.

While we as leaders still have to drive into the future, Stanley says it's not about making our mark on the world; it's about God making his mark through us.

If we settle this in our minds—that God is the one responsible for our leadership results—we will be in a perfect position for him to do what he wants through us.

> "Stand still & see this great thing the Lord is about to do before your eyes!" (1 Sam. 12:16) Wait for God's #leadership.

## Forget About Building a Legacy

If your goal in life is to build a memory of yourself and what you've done, how is that different from idolatry, which God hates?

We tend to define *legacy* as passing on the best of ourselves to the next generation. But when you analyze the mechanics of what that really means, you can't avoid the mental picture of erecting a selfie statue for the benefit of future adorers.

I struggle in this area with writing books. In the past I've envisioned people at my wake someday seeing a table full of them and marveling at what I accomplished in my life. This is my statue, an idol I must cast down. But I still feel called to write, and I am left with the spiritual tension this calling creates. I guess it's not much different for preachers, musicians, or other public performers who glorify God through their work on stage or at the podium.

For decades I wrote fantasy novels and thrillers that never got published. It was hugely frustrating, but I vowed to spend the rest of my life chipping away until I broke into print. I wanted fans! (Or "followers" in today's vernacular).

When I became a believer in my early twenties, I quickly realized I couldn't keep writing about the same stuff. None of it honored the Lord. My attitude about writing didn't either.

So I gave up the novel I was working on at the time and dedicated my future writing career to God.

I decided to focus on biblical principles. I made a commitment to encourage Christian leaders as well as reach non-Christians who have an appreciation—a curiosity, if you will—for what the ancient Scriptures say about leading people and running companies.

I still run the risk of God admonishing me for building my own name. This gives me pause when I write. It also makes me sad when I see ministry friends building themselves up, and it forces me to examine my own motivations.

This has driven me to build God's name into the pillar of my life. If you blog or write books or speak to groups, will you join me in this commitment?

> *I want to build others up. Build the next generation. Build ministries, friendships, my marriage. I want to do this by building my life on God's Word through the guidance of the Holy Spirit.*

It's OK to build knowledge, wisdom, and character—these are useful in God's economy and can themselves be passed on.

But let's stop obsessing about the "L" word. We're not here to build legacies; we're here to obey the Lord, love others, and leave a deposit for the next generation.

## CHAPTER 13

# Leadership Development

## Introduction

> "Don't conform any longer to the pattern of this world; be transformed by the renewing of your mind" (Rom. 12:2). #Leadership begins with renewal.

> "But we have the mind of Christ" (1 Cor. 2:16b). The #leadership mind should think differently with Christ than without.

Have you ever changed your mind about something important and wondered how you ever could've believed something so wrong?

I've flip-flopped on several issues. Before I became a Christ-follower in my early twenties, I believed abortion was OK. Now I'm vehemently against it. I used to believe in natural evolution but was convinced of God's creative power the minute I believed in Jesus. I used to think people were inherently good; now I know they're sinful to the core.

Has faith rocked your world too? I very much subscribed to the world's pattern of thought. But when God filled me with his Spirit, the first thing that changed in my life was my thinking. This helped me sin less and change my desires and habits. Inside-out transformation occurred in rapid fashion, as Paul describes in Romans:

> Don't copy the behavior and customs of this world, but let God transform you into a new person by changing the way you think. Then you will learn to know God's will for you, which is good and pleasing and perfect. (Rom. 12:2, NLT)

As our thinking changes, we find it easier to break from worldly ways. God's will then becomes more apparent as the fog lifts and we think his thoughts and hear his words.

In order for him to do this, we must find our identity in Jesus. This establishes our change: "[I]f anyone is in Christ, the new creation has come" (2 Cor. 5:17). We then receive the Holy Spirit, and we start regarding people and life from a spiritual perspective, causing us to act and think differently.

The Spirit whispers into the recreated mind intimate words, thoughts, impressions, and emotions. It's a beautiful thing!

Our personal development flows from this relationship. We start taking on Christ's likeness. And people notice.

I believe leaning into this personal development, and encouraging it in our followers, is the most important thing we can do as leaders. But what if we've been Christians for many years, with lots of leadership miles behind us? Is it ever too late to change?

Of course not. But it can be daunting to know where to start when your list of options includes character, personality, habits, dealing with failure, and numerous other areas of leadership.

The best place to begin is to grasp the fact that God knows us better than we do.

> "O Lord, you have searched me & you know me" (Ps. 139:1). Even when no one else understands me. #leadership

He knows our inner thoughts and desires, our faults and our wiring. He created us the way we are, and he made us for a specific purpose and plan. He has a process laid out of how he wants to change us. In today's jargon, this is "personal development" but the kind that goes to our core being, our very soul.

In this section, we will explore how to discover and implement the development plans he has for us.

> "According to the plan of him who works out every-thing in conformity with the purpose of his will" (Eph. 1:11). #Leadership is not my will, but his.

> "Set up the tabernacle according to the plan shown you on the mountain" (Exod. 26:30). Lord, show me your plan for my #leadership!

## Begin—and Stay—in the Word

One of the primary ways we hear from God is by reading the Bible. So many people wonder how they can know his will for their lives, and yet they never crack open his Word. Maybe it's because they believe it's just an ancient book with little to say about their life today. On the contrary:

> "The word of God is alive and active" (Heb. 4:12). So why not read it? #leadership

Strange to think of a book as alive. How is that possible?

**God's Word is more than words.** It is a person: "In the beginning was the Word, and the Word was with God, and the Word was God" (John 1:1).

**It is inspired.** "For prophecy never had its origin in the human will, but prophets, though human, spoke from God as they were carried along by the Holy Spirit" (2 Pet. 1:21).

**It is eternal.** "Heaven and earth will pass away, but my words will never pass away" (Matt. 24:35).

**It is perfect.** "And the words of the LORD are flawless, like silver purified in a crucible, like gold refined seven times" (Ps. 12:6).

**It convicts.** "It judges the thoughts and attitudes of the heart" (Heb. 4:12).

**It spreads.** "But the word of God continued to spread and flourish" (Acts 12:24).

**It clashes.** "Take the helmet of salvation and the sword of the Spirit, which is the word of God" (Eph. 6:17).

**It guides.** "Your word is a lamp for my feet, a light on my path" (Ps. 119:105).

The first step of any Christian leader's personal development plan should be a Bible reading regimen. The instructions are simple: Read every day; whenever you come across something that speaks to you, do what it says.

> "Do not merely listen to the word, and so deceive yourselves. Do what it says" (Jas. 1:22). Our #leadership mandate.

He replied, "Blessed rather are those who hear the word of God and obey it." (Luke 11:28)

If you've been a believer for a while, perhaps it's time to look at the Bible with fresh eyes. Here's something I tried that gave me a "wow" experience:

> Want to see the Bible in a new light? Read Revelation all the way through without slowing down for study. Mind-blowing. #leadership

Sometimes reading books of the Bible straight through can jumpstart a leader's spiritual life. When I do this, reading all the rich context enlightens the Word for me in a whole new way. If you're used to reading only a handful of verses at a time or hearing sermons that focus on short passages, this will be refreshing.

> "For we do not write you anything you cannot read or understand" (2 Cor. 1:13). The Bible is accessible. #leadership

If we want to develop our leadership and our life, we begin with the living book.

## Resist Culture

> Resist "human tradition & the basic principles of this world" & depend on Christ (Col. 2:8). #Leadership resists and depends.

Even as we dive into the Word, we must leave the world behind. Not that we should be cultural escapists and go live in a cave, but when we recognize the negative influence the world has on our spiritual lives, the only viable option is to resist its allure.

> "Save yourselves from this corrupt generation" (Acts 2:40). #Leadership is not bowing to popular culture.

Over time, the world, influenced by Satan, wants to enslave us. From childhood we are exposed to explicit images on the web, movies with explosive violence and language, and music that glorifies all the above. As we get older, a desire for riches, fame, and ease tempt us, and if we're not careful, the temptation shapes our leadership.

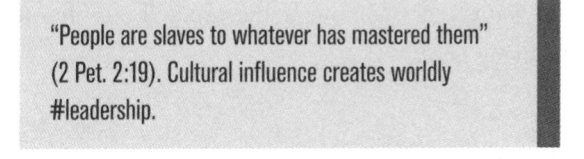

"People are slaves to whatever has mastered them" (2 Pet. 2:19). Cultural influence creates worldly #leadership.

How do we resist these influences? Paul says in Colossians 2:8 that we must depend on Christ. There's something else we should do:

"If anyone would come after me, he must deny himself" (Mark 8:34). #Leadership must reject self-gratification.

Culture wants us to gratify ourselves. Jesus wants us to deny ourselves.

In leadership, a practical way to deny ourselves is to practice humility.

## Discover True Humility

In today's marketplace, humble leadership is clichéd and over-done. At first it was a novel concept; then as it became secular-ized and its biblical origins ignored, many leaders simply started *acting* humble because it got results.

False humility is a pet peeve of mine. But I'm not so innocent myself. I've pretended to be humble while on the inside secretly enjoyed the attention. I'm sure you've done this at least once.

True humility is not easy to understand or practice. The humbling blocks are many. But there's a very convincing point that motivates me to try:

> Humbling yourself is easier to take than someone else doing it for you. #leadership

Boy, I've learned this one the hard way! When I've passed up an opportunity to keep my ego in check, the Lord has brought someone else along to save me from myself. Other times I'll make a mistake, misspeak, or in some way misstep so that I'm exposed and embarrassed.

The shame comes because I hope people view me as humble, and when they find out otherwise, I feel like a hypocrite and that I've brought disgrace to the faith and the Lord himself.

> My best #leadership development happens when God allows me to be humbled.

So the antidote becomes making sure I stay in my place.

> "Do not think of yourself more highly than you ought" (Rom. 12:3). #Leadership humility should be at the thought level.

> "There is no one righteous, not even one" (Rom. 3:10). #Leadership doesn't make a person superior in the eyes of God.

> "Whoever humbles himself like this child is the greatest in the kingdom of heaven" (Matt. 18:4). Humility leads to greatness. #leadership

Once we accept and process humility in our lives and in our leadership, I believe we're ready for the next step in our journey.

## Walk through Humility to Wisdom

> Though you may be in charge, "do not be wise in your own eyes" (Prov. 3:7). But be in charge!

Humility and wisdom together are two complementary forces that shape us and qualify us to lead. The Bible teaches that humility is wise, and the wise are humble.

If your position requires you to lead in a visible way, you can't help but be in front of people. How is this humble, you might ask? One answer is to emulate how Jesus entered the limelight but wisely kept walking through it toward a greater vision.

In our daily leadership, wisdom walks the fine line between pride and humility, dampening the former and strengthening the latter. The true servant leader employs wisdom to great effect while keeping God's vision for his or her life in full view.

The checklist below gives us further guidance from the Bible. The first list examines what foolish leaders do, and the second helps us recognize and develop leadership wisdom.

## What Makes Us Fools?

> "The sort of error that arises from a ruler: Fools are put in many high positions . . ." (Eccl. 10:5) #Leadership mistake #1.

As leaders, our first responsibility is to make sure we don't hire or appoint other foolish leaders. "Duh," I heard you say. Ah, but the Bible gives us some wise ways to help us evaluate candidates.

1. Does the leader believe in God?

> "The fool says in his heart, 'There is no God'" (Ps. 14:1). #Leadership without God isn't true leadership.

2. Does he or she talk too much?

> "Fools multiply words" (Eccl. 10:14). #Leadership antennae should be sensitive to verbosity.

> "The more the words, the less the meaning, & how does that profit anyone?" (Eccl. 6:11) Quiet #leadership is profitable.

3.  Does he or she thrive on quick, emotional intuition?

> "Desire without knowledge is not good—how much more will hasty feet miss the way!" (Prov. 19:2) #Leadership = informed zeal.

> "The discerning heart seeks knowledge, but the mouth of a fool feeds on folly" (Prov. 15:14). #Leadership is learning.

4.  Does he or she deal with symptoms or understand causes?

> We must look deeper as we lead. "You are looking only on the surface of things" (2 Cor. 10:7a).

5.  Does he or she thrive on conflict?

> "It is to one's honor to avoid strife, but every fool is quick to quarrel" (Prov. 20:3). PEACE in the office!

The challenge is to discern these character flaws in a potential leader before they're put into a position of authority. When we start observing these deficiencies in the leaders already on our team, rarely will we be able to stamp them out.

## What Makes Us Wise?

> Stay away from a fool, for you will not find knowledge on their lips. (Prov. 14:7)

The first rule of avoiding folly is to keep the fools at bay; conversely, the first rule of wisdom is to surround yourself with the wise.

> "He who walks with the wise grows wise" (Prov. 13:20). Osmosis #leadership development.

The following self-inventory questions will help point out what you might need to work on next in your personal quest for wisdom.

1.  Have I asked for wisdom?

> "Give your servant a discerning heart to govern your people" (1 Kgs. 3:9). A young king wanted wisdom before success. #leadership

> "Give me wisdom & knowledge that I may lead this people" (2 Chron. 1:10). Already a success, Solomon wanted more wisdom. #leadership

2. Do I act wisely?

> "Wisdom is proved right by her deeds" (Matt. 11:19). Jesus' #leadership was criticized, but his actions established him.

3. Do I measure my words?

> "When words are many, sin is not absent, but he who holds his tongue is wise" (Prov. 10:19). No long meetings!

> "A man who lacks judgment derides his neighbor, but a man of understanding holds his tongue" (Prov. 11:12).

4. Do I patiently look under the surface?

> "The purposes of a man's heart are deep waters; but a man of understanding draws them out" (Prov. 20:5). #Leadership goes behind the curtain.

> "A man's wisdom gives him patience; it is to his glory to overlook an offense" (Prov. 19:11). #Leadership sometimes overlooks.

5. Do I try too hard to understand God's ways?

> "God has mercy on whom he wants to have mercy & hardens whom he wants to harden" (Rom. 9:18). Our #leadership must bow to a mysterious God.

"As the heavens are higher than the earth, so are my ways higher than your ways and my thoughts than your thoughts" (Isa. 55:9).

This last point may be the wisest of all: No matter how much wisdom the Lord grants us, we will never understand all his ways.

Fortunately, his Word reveals what we need to know here and now.

## Find a Better Version of Yourself

You need to change something about your inborn leadership personality. I do too.

Could yours benefit from a jolt of energy or a blanket of calm? Perhaps a pinch more of humor or fewer crass jokes?

Our natural personalities are stubborn things. And they definitely aren't ideal. When we try to adopt the best qualities we see in others, our self-preservation instinct fights back. Not to mention, sin fuels our ego, fears, and selfish ambition. Only things like humility, obedience, and love will start us on the road to walking like Christ.

For it is *his* personality we should study and emulate. The Bible calls each of us to be more complete and mature versions of ourselves, while also taking on the personality of Christ.

We can remain true to our God-given style of leadership yet allow God's Word and the Holy Spirit to mold us into a new creation.

How we reconcile this tension is the sweet spot of godly leadership.

## Beware This Silent Leadership Killer

The crowd was so thick people were trampling each other. Yet before he addressed them, Jesus took his disciples aside for a few quick lessons.

The first is found in Luke 12:1b–3:

> Be on your guard against the yeast of the Pharisees, which is hypocrisy. There is nothing concealed that will not be disclosed, or hidden that will not be made known. What you have said in the dark will be heard in the daylight, and what you have whispered in the ear in the inner rooms will be proclaimed from the roofs.

Christ took that moment to teach his inner circle that though the masses see one version of us, a different one dwells within. Our sinful hearts create an inner self that looks after its own.

The self we let others see will usually be better than the real internal one, but Jesus wanted his lead team to close the gap between them. He wants the same for us.

His warning is stark: People will find out about you.

Watch what you say when you think no one can hear because it will get out. Watch what you watch because someone will walk in on you and glance at your screen. Watch what you think because it will register on your face.

When the gap between our inner and hypocritical outer selves widens, we tend to fall in.

## Don't Fall into the Authenticity Fallacy

I'm sure you've encountered the "authenticity" trend. Just be authentic, and people will love you. Share your feelings, embrace your emotion, reveal your faults, and you'll be a leader just like that.

> Depending on the #leadership context, there is a danger in being over-authentic.

But the fallacy is that sometimes I don't want my leader to be authentic—I just want him or her to tell me what to do. Sometimes I need them to be strong and do the hard stuff. It's cool that they're a real person, but if they tell me how tired or ill-equipped they feel, my confidence in their leadership will falter.

## Run from Your Habits into the Fire

Every leader has habits that drain his or her effectiveness. I'm not talking about parking in the same spot or drinking coffee at the same time every day; I'm referring to those bad habits that slow us down, embarrass us, impede our effectiveness, or hinder our leadership in some way.

I leave conversations too early. I don't ask enough questions. I avoid meetings. I don't finish a task before I glance at the squirrel going by. I don't spend enough social time with people. I hesitate to engage and probably come across as aloof.

So that's me. What about you? Do you speak too quickly, harshly, or voluminously? Do your emotions get the better of you?

The point is to identify your bad habits and work on them. If you and I want to grow as leaders, we can't allow our same old selves to define who we'll always be.

One reason God allows pain into our lives is to refine us and deepen us. He wants to conform us to the likeness of his Son. That's radical change.

> For you, God, tested us; you refined us like silver. (Ps. 66:10)

> Remove the dross from the silver, and a silversmith can produce a vessel. (Prov. 25:4)

The main ingredient of a silver forge isn't silver—it's fire. Lots of heat produces a little valuable, malleable, precious metal.

God will of course continue to refine us in ways we never could on our own. He works on the heart; we can work on obeying his Word and exercising self-control.

So as we try to control our tongues, eyes, and actions, let's allow the Lord to fashion us into beautiful silver vessels that he can use to pour out grace on those we lead.

Even if becoming silver hurts.

> "Each one should test their own actions" (Gal. 6:4).
> #Leadership begins with managing oneself.

## Fall in Behind the Faithful Centurion

> "I tell you, I have not found such great faith even in Israel."
>
> —*Luke 7:9*

My friend Dann Spader points to the centurion as a leader that impressed even Jesus. The story in Luke 7:1–10 shows us the character qualities of this amazing man.

- He "valued highly" his servant—rare for a Roman centurion (v. 2).
- He was a man's man, with a hundred men under him (v. 2).
- He "amazed" Jesus by his "great faith"—only said of two people in the Bible (v. 9).
- He was greatly respected by the religious leaders (v. 4).
- He loved Israel—rare for a Roman soldier (v. 5).

- He lived a generous lifestyle (v. 5).
- He had many other friends (v. 6).
- He was truly humble (v. 7).
- He understood how true authority works—rare even today (v. 8).
- He believed deeply (v. 10).

Though we never learn his name, Jesus points to him as someone living out the principles in the Sermon on the Mount.

This man embodied true spiritual leadership. Look at the above list one more time. What qualities do you need to work on? What leaders around you could benefit from studying this story in Scripture?

## Don't Just Be Yourself

Sergio De La Mora, lead pastor of Cornerstone Church of San Diego, said this in an *Outreach* magazine article in 2013:

> God distinctly told me to stop being the pastor I *wanted* to be and start becoming the pastor the community *needed* me to be. Though it was only one sentence, its ripple effect changed the course of our church forever.

This is true of leadership in general—we shouldn't just be the leader we aspire to be, but the leader our company, church, team, and family need us to be.

It's also true that situations and circumstances change, requiring us to lead differently, to be someone different. So how do I know who to be at any given moment? Must I catalog multiple personalities in my brain and call one up every time people need someone different? And shouldn't I just be myself, after all?

Scripture sets our thinking straight on this:

> Whoever claims to live in [God] must live as Jesus did. (1 John 2:6)

If we lead thousands or even no one at all, this command applies to us. We must imitate Christ as he walked and talked in this life. It's like stepping into his sandals while his feet are still in them.

If we walk like him, we can't help but start acting like him. After a while there should be a resemblance. If we are in him, we will lead like him, love like him, and live like him.

Who do people really need you to be as their leader? Do they need a different version of you depending on the day, or someone who acts like Jesus all the time?

## How Do You Build Yourself up as a Leader?

We've got to keep growing ourselves if we want our people to grow.

Do you read a lot of leadership books or go to conferences? Sometimes I feel like I read and study leadership too much. Whenever we do this, there's a danger that we aren't growing in practice—just in knowledge. And of course, knowledge by itself puffs up.

By far the best leadership development comes when we walk with the Holy Spirit, read the Word, and lean into the experiences he brings our way. If we only want to lead for the money, power, ego, or legacy, we are only serving ourselves and are in danger of being called least in the Kingdom.

Good leadership rarely emerges without a foundation of experience. But it never emerges—especially in the church—if the Holy Spirit isn't leading the leader.

As Paul says in Colossians 2:8, we must resist "human tradition and the elemental spiritual forces of this world" and depend on Christ.

When we depend on him, we know we're on the right path, and our followers will thank us for it.

# Four Bottlenecks That Are Choking Your Leadership

One thing all leaders must do is find and eliminate the bottlenecks in their organizations.

Depending on the number of people on staff or in volunteer roles, the bottleneck, of course, may be *you*. (But we won't go there.)

To be clear, a bottleneck is a choke point where the flow of work slows. It's a little more than a speedbump or a pile of debris in the road. It's like the organization's blood flow cuts off and muscles start to starve.

Here are four common bottlenecks that wage war against productivity, along with some questions to help you determine if they've snuck into your own organization.

**1. Projects**: Some projects keep getting delayed, demand more resources, cause conflict, or keep changing. Chances are you can name one right now that's been on your list for too many months.

- What would happen if it never got done? Can it be discontinued without jeopardizing the organization?
- Would people cheer if you killed it?

**2. Personalities**: Some people's personality differences won't go away. They'll do whatever they can to avoid each other or get at each other's throats, which can be a problem if they're on the same team, even just for a short-term project.

- Can you change things up so they don't have to work together?
- Have you had a frank talk with them separately?
- Does one of them need to go?

**3. Processes**: A process that hasn't been refined or rethought in a while tends to become an Untouchable. It turns into an obstacle on the path of productivity that people step over or around.

- What processes need review?
- What new processes should replace old ones?

**4. Politics**: This nasty little bottleneck can stifle an organization's effectiveness. When people constantly jockey for their own benefit, the leader starts to lose control.

- Who on your team is guilty of politicking? (Get their name[s] in your mind as you answer the next question.)
- When was the last time you confronted them about their conduct?

What other bottlenecks plague your workplace? Maybe it's time to ask some tough questions and get the blood flowing again.

## Care About What Others Think

> "For we are taking pains to do what is right in the eyes of the Lord and also in the eyes of men" (2 Cor. 8:21). We have an audience.

> "Be careful to do what is right in the eyes of everybody" (Rom. 12:17b). True #leadership integrity doesn't discriminate.

We know God sees everything we are and do, and we know he is the One to please above all others.

But people are watching too. And if they know we're Christians, shouldn't we be extra careful to also win their approval so as not to bring disrepute to God, whom we follow?

One of the ways to bear up under scrutiny is to handle money well.

> "Keep your lives free from the love of money & be content with what you have" (Heb. 13:5). Sometimes hard to do in #leadership.

> "Just as you excel in everything . . . see that you also excel in this grace of giving" (2 Cor. 8:7). A new kind of #leadership excellence.

We'll never know exactly who is watching, but it's safe to assume our audience of One is always present.

> Integrity is doing the right thing because God is watching. #leadership

## CHAPTER 14

# Joy and Peace

## Introduction

> A heart at peace gives life to the body,
> but envy rots the bones.
>
> —*Proverbs 14:30*

Isn't it interesting that Solomon chose to contrast peace with envy? When we're envious, we're stressing about what we don't have, whereas peace is content with whatever it has. When we envy, we covet, which is a sin; godliness with contentment is great gain (1 Tim. 6:6).

There is power in peace. It is a stress reducer, rejuvenator, life-producer. The absence of peace may indicate the absence of God's hand.

"There is no peace," says the LORD, "for the wicked."
(Isa. 48:22)

Peace is a precursor of joy. When we make peace with God, we taste his joy. When we make peace with people, reconciliation purifies our conscience and we find it easier to smile.

God wants us to be peaceful people at heart.

> "If it is possible, as far as it depends on you, live at peace with everyone" (Rom. 12:18). #Leadership strives for peace.

Blessed are the peacemakers, for they will be called children of God. (Matt. 5:9)

Love is peaceful.

Joy celebrates peace.

A peaceful soul finds rest in God.

> "May the Lord of peace himself give you peace at all times and in every way" (2 Thess. 3:16). My prayer as you struggle in #leadership.

## When Your Work Is Done, Quit

> "David returned home to bless his family" after his #leadership work was done (1 Chron. 16:43). A good example!

King David was spent. He had just come off a major leadership initiative that involved worship, singing, and staff reorganization. He had moved the holy ark of God to Jerusalem, its rightful home. Now it was time to go home himself and "bless his family."

Have you ever completed a huge undertaking or a major project and felt completely spent? Or maybe a heavy travel schedule kept you away from home, and you were ready to crash. This is a regular rhythm for me. Whether it's a writing project, speaking at conferences, or prepping to teach, I'm used to the build-up, explosion of energy, and postpartum blues.

Partly out of necessity, I have learned to regroup after spending myself. But I've also learned—more importantly—to regulate my energy during the surges so I have something left for family.

There's nothing worse than work getting the best of us, leaving us a worn-out shell for the people at home. They should be getting our best!

David, arguably the greatest king to walk the earth, knew how to peacefully ramp down after conquering enemies, establishing a country, and communing with God.

A great leadership example to follow.

## How to Fill Up with Joy

There are certain people that are just happy all the time. And then there's me. And probably you.

We have more ups and downs. More moods and attitudes. We're tired, wired, or just want to retire.

Too many of us rely on coffee to get us up in the morning and through the day. We grab a doughnut or some other sugar source to dampen the doldrums.

Beyond all the stimulants and pep talks, there is another source of energy and joy we can tap. God gives it to us in his Word.

> Those who look to him for help will be radiant with joy . . . (Ps. 34:5, NLT)

Relying on the Lord and walking closely with him add a certain quality to our countenance. Probably because when we do it, we are promised joy.

We also receive strength from that joy:

> The joy of the LORD is your strength. (Neh. 8:10c)

When we're down or grieve, he lifts us up with joy. When we need him, he loves us so much that he pours joy into us even before he helps us. *It's the act of trusting that bestows joy.*

Wanna feel more relaxed and happy with life and leadership? Employ joy.

> "... [l]ove, joy, peace, patience, kindness, goodness, faithfulness, gentleness and self-control" (Gal. 5:22). This is Spirit-led #leadership.

## Surprising Sources of Joy

> "This is the day the Lord has made; let us rejoice & be glad in it" (Ps. 118:24). Biblical #leadership is visionary & joyful.

What gives you joy in life? Chances are you know yourself pretty well and you do things that make you happy, whether vacations, daily rituals, hobbies, enjoyable work, serving, reading, or time with friends.

I'm sure you've experienced some hard things that brought even greater joy. Ever gone through a trial, a work challenge, a tough game, a project, or a final exam that stretched you to your limits? How did you feel when you emerged victorious?

There's a special joy on the other side of hardship (which is what heaven is all about!). We crave this joy in a spiritual sense. Jesus is our example:

> For the joy set before him he endured the cross, scorning its shame, and sat down at the right hand of the throne of God. (Heb. 12:2)

If Jesus willingly endured the equivalent of the electric chair because of the joy he knew waited on the other side, surely we can do the difficult things he's asking *us* to do!

To help us out, God provides several ways to get to his deep joy without leaving this life.

**Faith leads to joy.** When we first find faith and salvation, joy finds us as well:

> The jailer brought them into his house and set a meal before them; he was filled with joy because he had come to believe in God—he and his whole household. (Acts 16:34)

**Fear of the Lord leads to joy.** The right kind of fear is rooted in our love for the Lord. Because he is all-powerful, we never know what he's going to do, yet we are entirely sure of his love for us.

Imagine being among those who first saw the resurrected Christ.

> First people to see Jesus alive were "afraid yet filled with joy" (Matt. 28:8). This is what God-fearing #leadership looks like too!

**Work leads to joy.** We all search for fulfilling work throughout our lives, even after we reach retirement. We need purpose in life, and when we find work we love, we find a great blessing from above.

> "You are to rejoice before the Lord your God in everything you put your hand to" (Deut. 12:18b). Work is worship!

**Challenges lead to joy.** In 2 Corinthians 8:2, Paul commends the churches in Macedonia: "In the midst of a very severe trial, their overflowing joy and their extreme poverty welled up in rich generosity."

For these churches, trials, joy, and poverty led to overflowing generosity. How is that even possible? Perhaps they knew that without God's provision, they wouldn't be able to help themselves, let alone support missionaries.

Even when joy is doused by troubles, it perseveres. It morphed into generosity for the Macedonian churches.

With faith, fear of the Lord, meaningful work, and giving beyond our means, we will never be short on joy.

## CHAPTER 15

# The Leader's Deeper Spiritual Life

## Introduction

> I do believe; help me overcome my unbelief!
> —Mark 9:24

Many of us disentangle the secular from the spiritual, even if just a little. Whether it's a lack of belief that prayer works, the Holy Spirit speaks, or the Word is alive, when we enter work mode it's not hard for us to slip into some version of unbelief.

> "We have not even heard that there is a Holy Spirit" (Acts 19:2). Too many Christians could say the same.

Christian leadership requires constant spiritual input. This is why I try to pray or read the Bible before I start my work day. If I miss a day or two, it creates a sense of distance.

When I've pulled away from God, the secular creeps back into my thinking. I rely on my own strengths, pray less, and feel less compassionate (among other things.)

Come near to God and he will come near to you. (Jas. 4:8)

Part of the solution is getting close to the Lord through regular reading, praying, worshiping, and faith practicing. I say "practicing" because the more we do something, the better we get at it. Faith itself comes from God, but it is also a muscle that must be exercised to be effective.

> "To the faithful you show yourself faithful" (2 Sam. 22:26). We are faithful first, then he responds. #Leadership goes first.

As we lead, then, we must never lose sight of the unseen inner world of the Spirit. He is our leader, provider, protector, refiner—our everything.

## Work at His Whim

The longer I live and lead, the more I realize I'm doing both at the pleasure of the Lord.

> "People's lives are not their own; it is not for them to direct their steps" (Jer. 10:23). #Leadership is walking in reliance.

In many places the Bible reminds us who God is and who we are. He is the reason we're even alive. As Acts 17:28 says, "For in him we live and move and have our being."

Not to depress you, but that company or that church you've built? He did it. And all that money? From his hand, not anything special you've done.

> You may say to yourself, "My power and the strength of my hands have produced this wealth for me." But remember the LORD your God, for it is he who gives you the ability to produce wealth . . . (Deut. 8:17–18)

God is full of unending riches and power. Why should money be an obstacle to him when he already owns the whole earth?

> "God's voice was like the roar of rushing waters, and the land was radiant with his glory" (Ezek. 43:2). What is OUR #leadership in comparison?

When I read verses like this, I am overwhelmed by his greatness. His voice is a flood; his glory shines brighter than the sunniest day.

> "Now to the King eternal, immortal, invisible, the only God, be honor and glory for ever and ever. Amen" (1 Tim. 1:17). Only 1 king!

> "Holy, holy, holy is the LORD Almighty; the whole earth is full of his glory" (Isa. 6:3). #Leadership is bowing to glory.

There are too many verses about God's majesty to include here. With his glory firmly in mind, let's put him in his rightful place and wonder at his unsearchable splendor.

And then let's thank him for stooping down to our low level and caring about what we do. Even more than that, for giving us divine purpose.

> "Establish the work of our hands for us" (Ps. 90:17).
> God makes work meaningful. #leadership

## Worship Him

> "I will not sacrifice to the Lord burnt offerings that
> cost me nothing" (2 Sam. 24:24). Worship is more
> than a nod. #leadership

If we live in true relationship with someone, they are the first person we call when big things happen. We text them to see how they're doing. We get regular face time. Their opinion matters more than anyone else's.

If we are in relationship with God, we communicate with him in a similar way. But on top of that, we worship him—a type of "communication" we don't even have with our own spouse.

We worship him because he loves us like the perfect Father he is. He loves us so much he always delivers on his promises:

> "Not one of all the Lord's good promises to Israel
> failed; every one was fulfilled" (Josh. 21:45). #lead-
> ership #trust

There are so many aspects of his character that are perfect—his love chief among them.

It is why we worship him.

As you go about your day, consider the following ways to adore your Father.

**Anticipate him.** "As lightning that comes from the east is visible even in the west, so will be the coming of the Son of Man" (Matt. 24:27). We look forward to that day when Jesus returns as the reigning King.

**Seek his power.** Our faith awakens his will within our own, accomplishing our desires. "May he give you the power to accomplish all the good things your faith prompts you to do" (2 Thess. 1:11b, NLT).

**Cry out occasionally.** When we hurt, God cares.

> "Because you wept in my presence, I have heard you" (2 Kgs. 22:19). Humbling ourselves & crying out bends God's ear. #leadership

**Pray as you go.** Try it!

> "Then I prayed to the God of heaven, and I answered the king . . ." (Neh. 2:4–5) #Leadership seeks the Lord in mid-sentence.

**Confidently trust.** "Now faith is being sure of what we hope for and certain of what we do not see" (Heb. 11:1). Relying on the Lord builds joy, peace, and security.

> "May the God of hope fill you with all joy & peace as you trust in him" (Rom. 15:13). A #leadership blessing for you.

> "It is better to take refuge in the Lord than to trust in humans" (Ps. 118:8). There is only one infallible Leader.

## Be More Than What You Do

One morning after a meeting at church, I got in my car and prepared to head to the office. But before I started the car, I paused.

There was a mass of birds in the trees. Their calls mixed with the rustling leaves, and for a moment I rested my ears and listened.

Then I heard the whooshing traffic of a nearby expressway. The natural and man-made sounds mixed for a moment, each jockeying for prominence.

The contrast yielded a thought that seemed to come from God. It was as if he said, "Those people rushing by are in a hurry to do and go. Those birds are just being birds, enjoying their perches on this cool morning."

I had just finished a long-term writing project, so my energy was low. So many months of pushing, agonizing, praying, and sleeplessness had spent all my stores. I relished moments like this.

I felt no obligation to join the flow of traffic just yet. I wanted to chew on this scene and let the Lord soak my mind in his thoughts. I wasn't quite ready to leave this sanctuary.

"Just be my child," the Lord impressed upon me. He wanted me to stop churning. I felt him fill me with his presence in the space left empty by all my striving. I spent a couple minutes just listening, resting, being.

With his peace slowing my movements, I finally turned the ignition.

I joined the traffic and engaged the day, conscious of God's encouragement to *be*.

> "Since everything will be destroyed, what kind of people ought you to be?" (2 Pet. 3:11) It's not the building, it's the being.

## Emulate the Faith of Eva the Cab Driver

One morning when I hailed an airport cab in Miami, I looked forward to twenty-five minutes of staring out the window.

"Good morning!" the driver said with a broad smile and cheery voice. It took me a minute to process her good mood. No taxi driver had ever exhibited such joy upon my entrance.

Eva was a fifty-five-year-old Haitian with long dreadlocks and a thick accent. When she talked to the taxi company's home base, it sounded like she spoke French laced with Island dialect.

I found it hard to believe that her daughter hated her, but that's how Eva began her life story as she pulled into traffic.

After her own "mom-mom" had died thirteen years earlier, Eva felt little desire to visit the cemetery. She intensified her smoking habit and went through two cartons of Newports every day. One morning she had the distinct premonition that she would die soon herself.

She cried out to God to break her addiction before it buried her. "God, if you save me, I will serve you!"

During that night's fitful sleep, she said a "big voice" spoke to her. She knew it was God. He asked her if she remembered what she had done the day before. She didn't. The agitated dreaming resumed, now peppered with confusion.

The next day delivered more depression and smoke. Then, she said, it was as if someone grabbed the back of her head and forced her to fall back asleep.

This time the voice filled her dream with power and clarity. He told her she couldn't remember what she'd done the day before because of how she was living. He said he would save her from that addiction and indeed use her life in his service.

Her joy overflowed as she explained to me how he had used her since that day.

"I speak about him on the streets. Sometimes I don't know what to say. He speaks through me." Eva said every year she goes home to Haiti to share Jesus with people in the villages near her old home, in the midst of a sea of voodoo. One time there were about 300 people in the crowd, and more than half of them responded positively to her message.

"People come up to me afterward and say they want to know this God I talk about. But when that happens, I am amazed because I don't remember what I said! God's words flow through me, and sometimes I don't understand them."

We didn't have time to talk about her church upbringing, and I didn't sense there was any formal theological training in her background.

But there was joy and power.

And a faith that humbled me.

# Conclusion:
# Friends and Brothers

A few years ago, I had the opportunity to befriend Governor Matt Bevin of Kentucky. When talking to one of his young sons, I was amazed at the maturity of this boy and the way he saw his dad as a father more than a governor. He seemed unimpressed with the office but enamored with the man. Boy, did that speak to me as a dad and a leader!

I, too, must remember that my position is unimpressive to my family and friends. God is the One with the superior position and power. I am his servant. He has given me an assignment to lead a small number of people and to shepherd my family.

But I can't do it alone, and you can't either. This is why God has deposited the Holy Spirit in us. It's why he wants us to pray to him and walk with him. It's why we have a living example of godly leadership in his Son.

"The Son is the radiance of God's glory & the exact representation of his being" (Heb. 1:3). Why Jesus' #leadership was perfect.

While we are surrounded and indwelt by the divine, we must also be on the lookout for earthly friends the Lord may bring across our path.

"Hushai the Arkite was the king's friend" (1 Chron. 27:33). Do you have a friend supporting your #leadership?

I hope you have someone you can confide in. Someone close who knows you. It could even be a small group of confidants or accountability partners.

True friends are like family—they love us despite our title, success, power, or ego. They support us through our embarrassments and disappointments.

A friend loves at all times, and a brother is born for a time of adversity. (Prov. 17:17)

One who has unreliable friends soon comes to ruin, but there is a friend who sticks closer than a brother. (Prov. 18:24)

Jesus wants to be your best friend, closer even than family. His desire for relationship is so strong that he willingly died to defeat the sin that tugs at you, the enemy that nips at you, and the death that ultimately claims us all.

> Greater love has no one than this: to lay down one's life for one's friends. (John 15:13)

By rising again, he has pushed open the doors of eternity. And now he beckons us to live life to the fullest.

I hope and pray this book has encouraged you to confidently lead as a servant of the all-powerful Lord. That's how Jesus led, and as your closest friend, he wants to help you do the same.

> You are my friends if you do what I command. (John 15:14)

Now let's go lead in his strength.

# For Further Study

As I mentioned at the beginning of this book, the micro-devotions and Scriptures appearing on almost every page have been collected into one spot at **www.ServantLeaderStrong. com**. You can read, share, print, or use them in any way you like.

I would suggest copying the ones that stood out to you and pasting them into a separate document that you can reference in the future. If you're the social type, most of the devotional snippets will fit into individual posts on your favorite platform. I posted them all on Twitter myself a few years ago.

Finally, there is no substitute for your own personal reading of Scripture. Get a translation of your liking and start in the book of Proverbs. The leadership wisdom it contains is unsurpassed by any other book in existence.

# Acknowledgments

In Philippians 4:9, Paul says, "Whatever you have learned or received or heard from me, or seen in me—put it into practice. And the God of peace will be with you."

I have been blessed by many godly leaders throughout my life—too many to name. I've put into practice much of what they've taught me. Their lessons appear in this book and elsewhere.

Through all their positive influences and encouragement, I have felt the God of peace with me. I can recall many times his presence strengthened and sustained me.

My wife, Karen, has also encouraged me when I've traversed the valley. Often, as we've walked in lockstep, we've seen the Lord work in our marriage and family in surprising ways.

Whatever challenges you face in your servant leadership journey, I pray you will feel the Father's peaceful presence and hear his Word encouraging you to be strong and courageous.

Also, hear his promise in the verse above—that he *will* be with you as you put his words into practice.

# About the Author

**Tom Harper** has helped launch industry associations, parachurch ministry startups, and media companies. His passion for leadership inspired him to found BiblicalLeadership.com, a website offering free content and resources for Christian leaders. His other books include the business fable *Through Colored Glasses: How Great Leaders Reveal Reality* (DeepWater, 2018), *Leading from the Lions' Den: 66 Leadership Principles from Every Book of the Bible* (B&H, 2010), and *Career Crossover: Leaving the Marketplace for Ministry* (B&H, 2007). He and his family live near Louisville, Kentucky, and attend Southeast Christian Church.

Connect with Tom:
linkedin.com/in/tomrharper
twitter.com/TomRHarper